Learn Design for iOS Development

Sian Morson

Apress®

Learn Design for iOS Development

ISBN-13 (pbk): 978-1-4302-6364-7

ISBN-13 (electronic): 978-1-4302-6365-4

Trademarked names, logos, and images may appear in this book. Rather than use a trademark symbol with every occurrence of a trademarked name, logo, or image we use the names, logos, and images only in an editorial fashion and to the benefit of the trademark owner, with no intention of infringement of the trademark.

The use in this publication of trade names, trademarks, service marks, and similar terms, even if they are not identified as such, is not to be taken as an expression of opinion as to whether or not they are subject to proprietary rights.

While the advice and information in this book are believed to be true and accurate at the date of publication, neither the authors nor the editors nor the publisher can accept any legal responsibility for any errors or omissions that may be made. The publisher makes no warranty, express or implied, with respect to the material contained herein.

President and Publisher: Paul Manning
Lead Editor: Steve Anglin
Technical Reviewer: Danny Swarzman
Developmental Editor: Anne Marie Walker
Editorial Board: Steve Anglin, Mark Beckner, Ewan Buckingham, Gary Cornell, Louise Corrigan, Jim DeWolf, Jonathan Gennick, Jonathan Hassell, Robert Hutchinson, Michelle Lowman, James Markham, Matthew Moodie, Jeff Olson, Jeffrey Pepper, Douglas Pundick, Ben Renow-Clarke, Dominic Shakeshaft, Gwenan Spearing, Matt Wade, Steve Weiss
Coordinating Editor: Kevin Shea
Copy Editor: Karen Jameson
Compositor: SPi Global
Indexer: SPi Global
Artist: SPi Global
Cover Designer: Anna Ishchenko

Distributed to the book trade worldwide by Springer Science+Business Media New York, 233 Spring Street, 6th Floor, New York, NY 10013. Phone 1-800-SPRINGER, fax (201) 348-4505, e-mail orders-ny@springer-sbm.com, or visit www.springeronline.com. Apress Media, LLC is a California LLC and the sole member (owner) is Springer Science + Business Media Finance Inc (SSBM Finance Inc). SSBM Finance Inc is a Delaware corporation.

For information on translations, please e-mail rights@apress.com, or visit www.apress.com.

Apress and friends of ED books may be purchased in bulk for academic, corporate, or promotional use. eBook versions and licenses are also available for most titles. For more information, reference our Special Bulk Sales–eBook Licensing web page at www.apress.com/bulk-sales.

Any source code or other supplementary material referenced by the author in this text is available to readers at www.apress.com. For detailed information about how to locate your book's source code, go to www.apress.com/source-code/.

To Family, Friends and Al

Contents at a Glance

About the Author xv

About the Technical Reviewer xvii

Acknowledgments xix

Introduction xxi

■Chapter 1: So You've Got an Idea for an iPhone App, Now What? 1

■Chapter 2: iOS: What You Need to Know 9

■Chapter 3: iOS 7 and Flat Design 29

■Chapter 4: Getting to Know the User Interface of the iPhone and iPad
Design Considerations 39

■Chapter 5: Mobile Design Patterns 55

■Chapter 6: Using Wireframes to Design Your App 69

■Chapter 7: Designing Your Visual Assets with Adobe Photoshop 85

■Chapter 8: Creating Your App Icon and Additional Graphics for the App Store 103

■Chapter 9: Finalizing Your Assets for App Development 113

■Chapter 10: Design Best Practices and Mistakes to Avoid 127

Index 133

Contents

About the Author xv

About the Technical Reviewer xvii

Acknowledgments xix

Introduction xxi

■Chapter 1: So You've Got an Idea for an iPhone App, Now What? 1

Assumptions 2

    Step One: Define your idea 2

    Step Two: Share your idea with peers 3

    Step Three: Compare your app to others' 4

    Step Four: Analyze your findings 6

    Step Five: Store comparative apps for future reference 7

    Step Six: Revise your idea if needed 7

Summary 8

■Chapter 2: iOS: What You Need to Know 9

What to Expect in iOS 7 9

    iOS 7 Guiding Principles 10

Springboard 11

Typography 12

Icons 13

Bars 15

    Status Bar 16

    Navigation Bar 17

    Toolbar 17

    Tab Bar 18

Table Views and Table View Elements 18

    Table View Elements 20

Stock Apps 21

    Mail 22

    Calculator 22

    Calendar 23

    Weather 24

    Color, Transparency, & Layers 26

Buttons 28

Summary 28

Chapter 3: iOS 7 and Flat Design 29

The Principles of Flat Design 29

The Origin of and Other Uses of Flat Design 30

The Future of Flat Design 31

Incorporating Flat Design into Your App 31

    Choosing a Color Palette 32

    Designing Icons 33

    Utilizing Space and Templates 34

    Defining Buttons 34

    Simplifying Forms 36

    Determining Typography 37

    Evaluating Usability 38

Summary 38

■Chapter 4: Getting to Know the User Interface of the iPhone and iPad
Design Considerations 39

Use of Gestures in the UI 40

Consistency of Gestures 41

Direct Manipulation of Gestures 41

Abstract Gestures and Feedback 41

Gestures in iOS 43

Tap 43

Double Tap 43

Drag or Pan 44

Flick 44

Swipe 44

Pinch 44

Touch and Hold 44

Shake 44

New iOS Gestures 44

Swipe Up 45

Swipe Down 45

Swipe Right (In Mail App) 46

The iPad; How Is It Different? 46

Popover View 48

Split View Screen 49

Visual Context 50

User Interaction 50

Onscreen Targets 50

Screen Resolution 50

Universal Apps 51

Icons 51

App Icons 52

Launch Image 52

iPad-Specific Gestures 53

Summary 54

Chapter 5: Mobile Design Patterns 55

Registration & Login/Sign-up Forms 56

App Navigation 57

　Springboard or Home Screen Patterns...58

List & Table View Patterns 59

Tables..59

　Tabs 60

　Slide-Out Navigation..61

　Image Gallery 62

Searching and Sorting..62

Tips, Tours, and Walkthroughs..64

Stepping Out of the Box 66

Summary...67

Chapter 6: Using Wireframes to Design Your App 69

What Is a Wireframe?..69

　Tools for Wireframing 71

　Why Are Wireframes Important?...72

The Wireframing Process 72

　Focus on Usability 74

　Try Various Layouts...75

　Outline User Flow 75

　Define Use Cases..80

　Add Wireframe Details..81

　Share Wireframes for Feedback 81

　Create Prototypes 82

　Clients and Wireframes 83

Summary...84

Chapter 7: Designing Your Visual Assets with Adobe Photoshop...................85

Some Photoshop Basics 85

    Prepping for Retina..86

    Your Photoshop Setup 87

Gridlines & Guides 88

The Tools Panel 89

    Selection Tools...90

    Crop and Slice Tools 91

    Measuring Tools 91

    Retouching Tools 91

    Painting Tools 92

    Draw & Type Tools..92

    View and Navigation Tools 93

    3D Tools 93

The Layers Panel 93

Creating the Registration/Sign-in Page 95

Creating the Select and Edit Trips Page 98

Using Layer Comps for Screen Layouts...100

What about Adobe Fireworks? 101

Summary..102

Chapter 8: Creating Your App Icon and Additional Graphics for the App Store 103

App Discovery 103

The App Store 104

The App Icon 106

Launch Images 107

Newsstand Cover Icon..107

Promotional Screenshots 108

Promotional Artwork..110

Your App's Page 111

Summary..112

Chapter 9: Finalizing Your Assets for App Development 113

Creating a Design Specifications Document for Your Developer 114

Design Specifications Document Overview 114

Provide Color Information 114

Specify Fonts & Types 114

Explain User Interaction 115

Slicing Your Designs into Assets 117

Scaling and Saving Your Assets for Various Devices 122

Other Asset Preparation Tools 122

Naming Your Assets 123

Packaging Your Assets for Development 124

Communication Is Key 124

Summary 125

Chapter 10: Design Best Practices and Mistakes to Avoid 127

Create an App Design Statement 127

The HIG Is Your Design Bible; Use It 128

Wireframing Is Important 128

UI vs. UX: There Is a Difference 129

Simplify! 129

Utilize White Space 129

Be Aware of Changes to iOS 7 129

Ask Why? 129

Think Small 129

The iPad Isn't Just a Big iPhone 130

Fonts Are Important 130

Provide Visual Feedback 130

The User Is King (or Queen) 131

Design Patterns Are Your Friend 131

Thumbs Rule 131

Hi- to Low-Res 131

Get 'Em in Quick 131

Test, Test, and Test Again...132

Software Will Help 132

Icons and Screenshots Are Important, Too 132

Handoff and Communication...132

Summary..132

Index...133

About the Author

Sian Morson is a tech entrepreneur, mobile evangelist, and strategist.

In 2010, Sian founded Kollective Mobile to help businesses and startups with mobile development and strategy. A seasoned digital professional, Sian has worked with many high-profile clients to deliver large web builds and campaigns for popular brands. Her diverse skill set includes marketing, advertising, mobile strategy, business management, and thought leadership. She works closely with her partners and clients to assist them in achieving their overall business objectives.

Sian speaks and writes about mobile strategy for a number of publications and also works with a variety of nonprofits working to bridge the digital divide.

An internationally exhibited artist, Sian enjoys fusing her creativity with technology. Her video artwork has been featured in the prestigious Optica Festival in Spain; Director's Lounge Berlin; Aakriti Gallery in Mumbai, India; and MoCADA Museum in Brooklyn, New York.

About the Technical Reviewer

Danny Swarzman is a software engineer who has been developing software for Apple products since the Apple II. He has written many magazine articles about various computer systems both for professional programmers and for beginners. He is an electronics hobbyist who has developed sketches and interfaces for Arduino. Throughout his career he has created software to control conveyor systems, medical equipment, milling machines and various custom devices. When not developing software, he enjoys the occasional game of go. His email is danny at stowlake dot com. His site is `http://stowlake.com`.

Acknowledgments

To everyone at Apress: Kevin and James, thanks for your patience. Maybe the next one will be easier! Dominic and Steve, thank you for working with me to craft the initial outline for what this book eventually became. To all of the talented editors (Danny and Anne Marie) who helped to craft my ramblings into something coherent, I appreciate your help throughout this process. It's one of the hardest things I've ever done and certainly would not have been possible without you.

To all of the talented designers and developers at Kollective Mobile, thank you for helping to make my job infinitely easier. And thank you to my designer friend and colleagues who have inspired me with their work: Drew, Ryland, Henry & Mike.

Lastly, to those who supported me when I didn't think I could do it: Mom, Alison, Khem and Lisa – thank you all for your support.

Introduction

iOS is one the most popular mobile operating systems of our time. If you are serious about mobile design, then iOS 7 is a must. As the owner of a mobile development agency, I can tell you that over 50 percent of our requests for apps are requested for iOS. With the release of iOS 7 and new devices, iOS is a global leader in a mobile ecosystem. Anyone serious about mobile design or development cannot exclude iOS.

Who This Book Is For

This book is for those already familiar with iOS from a development standpoint but are now ready to try their hand at design. It assumes that you are familiar with some of the nuances of the operating system and are interested in designing a simple application that either you or someone else will develop. The book will take you through the process of crafting your idea into a clear and actionable statement, through the details of creating your first wireframes and ultimately to design your app. It highlights tools and tips to help you with the design process and even highlights popular mobile design patterns to ease some of the challenges of design. If you're ready to take on designing for the world's most popular mobile operating system, Learn Design for iOS is for you.

How to Use This Book

This book is structured in a way that allows you to take your concept for an iOS application from your initial idea through preparation for development. The book will guide you, step-by-step through the processes of idea validation, ideation, design, and asset preparation for development. It covers creation of screens and guidelines that designers should be aware of from Apple's Human Interface Guidelines. The book is a general high-level guide for those who are interested in learning more about the iPhone operating system and what is required when designing an application for the iPhone, iPod Touch, or iPad.

What You'll Find on the Web Site

The apress.com web site contains a sample Design Specifications document for the fictional Travel Light application referred to in the book. It provides a guide on which fonts, colors, and other information that the developer needs to know during development of the application.

Chapter 1

So You've Got an Idea for an iPhone App, Now What?

Congratulations! You've got an idea for an app and have made the important decision to design it yourself! You've joined the ranks of the hundreds of thousands who have decided to learn just what is required to take an idea from a tiny spark in your imagination to a fully designed application ready for development.

As you may or may not already know, apps are an integral part of the mobile ecosystem. All mobile devices run apps. However, your decision to design an app for iOS is a unique one. Of all of the app stores, the Apple app store is the granddaddy of them all, featuring more apps than any other app store. But, you already know this because you've chosen to design an app for iOS.

Apps are everywhere. Since the Apple app store initially launched in July 2008 with 500 apps, the number of apps have increased steadily. As of June 2013, that number has increased to just under 900,000 with Apple CEO Tim Cook estimating that $10 billion has been paid out to developers so far. So, if you have an idea for an app, there are great opportunities for making money and reaching a large audience with it. Those are pretty good reasons for wanting to design for iOS.

These days, ideas for apps aren't hard to find. Lots of people have them. So, how do you take your idea from just an idea to creating an actual app that is in the app store and runs on a device? It doesn't happen overnight, but with a little diligence, it's absolutely possible.

Getting an app into Apple's app store isn't the hard part. But creating an app that features an original idea, great visuals, and great execution is; it requires lots of planning, a bit of research, and some dedication.

If you are to take your idea through from just an idea to a fully designed and developed iOS app running on mobile devices, there are steps that you will need to take to get it there: very specific ones.

While the process itself might seem arduous it is a necessary one, especially if this is your first time attempting to design the app.

The simple truth is that most apps that are submitted to the app store die on the vine and fall into obscurity shortly after their release date. Without proper planning and faced with the competition from the sheer number of other apps in the app store, if your app doesn't feature a unique idea and execution, then chances are, it won't be noticed by very many people. Whether it's for business or just a personal project, your ultimate goal when thinking of creating an app is to reach as many people as possible. If you've got a great idea for an app and you believe in it, then do it. There are many people who come up with an idea and never take it anywhere so you're a part of a very small minority simply by having that idea. Celebrate it because the real work starts now.

Assumptions

This book makes a few assumptions, the main one being that you are at the very least familiar with iOS from a development standpoint but are looking for an opportunity to expand your development knowledge with some design knowledge as well. This book, however, is not about development per se. If you are curious about learning how to *build* an iPhone app, then this book isn't for you. If you are, however, looking to enhance your knowledge of design specifically as it relates to the iPhone operating system, then you are in the right place.

For the purposes of simplicity, in this chapter I've broken out the ideation process into six easy-to-follow steps. Each step will bring you closer to the ultimate goal of designing your iOS app.

1. Define your idea.

2. Share your idea with peers.

3. Compare your app to others'.

4. Analyze your findings.

5. Store comparative apps for future reference.

6. Revise your idea if needed.

Step One: Define your idea

First, write down your idea in one or two sentences. Three might be permissible but really try to nail it in two short sentences. If you need more sentences, that's fine; however, the goal is to be able to describe and explain the idea behind your app and what it does in 30 seconds or less. This is usually called your elevator pitch and it is the first step in the process. Spend some time trying to make the sentence or sentences as succinct as possible while still capturing what your app does. This is important and will serve you and your app as you move forward because you will return to these statements again and again as you design and ultimately build your application. As you move through the next few steps, you will find that your description of the app might change as you look at other apps and categories. This is a natural part of the process. Be flexible and open to change.

For example: "The Travel Light app will help frequent travelers by providing checklists to ensure that they pack only what they need for their upcoming trips."

After you've written your statement out, recite it until you have it in your memory. You should be able to say it without referring back to your notes. Ask yourself how it sounds. Are you using proper grammar? Are your ideas about the application timely? Does it solve a problem that people are facing today? Does it address issues in a way that people need it to? Is it unique? If so, what is unique about it? If not, then you will need to keep working on your description. Don't rush this process. If you get stuck on the first step, then it is likely that your idea needs some work. Give it the time that it deserves.

Once you can clear this first hurdle and you are happy with your description of the app, set it all aside and return to it after a few days. When you read your idea and its description again, does it sound as exciting to you as it did the first time? Does the sentence make you want to explore the application further? What has changed? More importantly, does it still sound like a good idea, and does it still fill you with the passion you initially had for the project?

If not, then it might be worth it to take another stab at your description and the idea that spawned it. Depending on how strongly you feel about it, you might want to scrap that idea altogether and start on another idea for a different app. It is all up to you.

It is important to remember that many people have ideas every day. But, there's a big difference between having an idea and actually bringing it to fruition. The first step in the process is moving your idea past the initial idea stage.

But, if you feel just as strongly as you did at the beginning and are still passionate about your idea, then it's time to progress to the next step.

Step Two: Share your idea with peers

Share your idea with others! This might sound counterintuitive and even downright scary to some, but it's really not. In order to validate your idea, you simply must share it with others. What good is an idea if it sits in your head? Ask your friends and others around you that you trust and get them to speak honestly in response to your idea. Try to share your idea and description with people who aren't afraid to give you honest feedback. Ask for constructive criticism, but also be sure that you are ready to receive it.

Ask questions that will help to move the idea forward and ultimately inform its design and functionality. If you have time, create a brief questionnaire and ask people to fill it out.

Staying with our initial idea of a Travel Light app above, the following questions are examples of what you might ask:

1. Do you understand the problem the app is trying to solve?

2. If not, what's missing?

3. Is it clear to whom the app is trying to reach?

4. Would you use this app? Why or why not?

5. What would you change?

Briefly state the idea around the app, what it does, and how it will work. Then ask a few key questions that will help to provide you with information that will help to develop the idea further.

The questions should be leading with the intent of drawing responses that are as specific as possible. At this point in the ideation process, the more specific the responses, the more valuable they will be to you and will help to inform the design of your application.

Some of you might be hesitant to share your ideas with others at this stage. In this day and age of patent trolls and copyright infringements, it might be easy to think that sharing your idea is the wrong thing to do. Remember, you can't copyright an idea so it is important to get critical feedback up front and early in the process. If you are concerned about sharing your ideas with a wider audience, stick with a core group of people that you can trust. Friends, colleagues, and even family members will do as long as they are within the target demographic for your app.

The process doesn't have to be a long, drawn-out affair either. Your description of the app and what it does and a few short questions that will illicit the best feedback will suffice.

Once you've done this and you receive responses either verbally or via your questionnaire, go through all responses carefully. Are the answers clear? Do you need to ask follow-up questions for clarification? If you need to, then do so. When this is complete, sit down with your idea and the feedback you've received and review your idea description while reviewing the feedback. How can you revise your idea to address the issues outlined in the feedback?

It is important to note that not all feedback is good feedback. Some feedback, you will need to take with a grain of salt. A good rule of thumb is to consider feedback and suggestions that bring you closer to the core of what you saw your app to be. If the feedback you receive helps you to solve the problem your app is addressing, then consider it. Did you receive feedback that was unexpected or that might cause you to rethink your idea? This is perfectly fine.

If you need to rewrite your statement and description for your idea, then do so and check it against the feedback you've received again. Keep all the feedback you receive, even if you don't use it in this phase of the project. It will come in handy later as you move through the design process.

Step Three: Compare your app to others'

In this step, we will begin to really expand on the initial idea you created for your app in step 1. Now that you've validated it with a small control group of potential users, we'll need to see how your idea stands up against existing apps in the Apple app store.

Since the App store launched in 2008 with 500 apps, the number of applications available for iOS devices has grown exponentially every year. As mentioned earlier, as of June 2013, there were approximately 900,000 apps in the Apple app store. That's a lot of competition! Luckily, Apple does a pretty good job at categorizing the apps, and the app store is easy to access and browse right from your iPhone, iPad, or iPod Touch.

A good place to start is in the Featured section or tab of the App store. Here, you will see the New and Noteworthy and What's Hot sections of the store. These are apps that have been chosen by Apple's editorial staff as exhibiting best-in-class usability, design, and functionality. Because of this, they are featured by Apple and also tend to do extremely well when it comes to popularity and sales. Usually, these apps are flagged upon submission to the app store as being unique. Apple's editorial staff tries to pick apps that are innovative in some way to feature in the App store. Chances are, you may already have some of these apps but with the sheer number of apps being released every day, you may see new apps that you've not seen before. Apps in the New and Noteworthy and What's Hot sections will be from a variety of categories. It is a good idea to view apps that aren't in your particular app's category as well as ones that are to be able to see a variety of styles and functionalities.

Take a look at apps in the Top Charts as well for an indication of which apps are currently most popular. Navigate to each app's page and pay particular attention to the description and screenshots for each app. Are there any hints as to what makes this app unique in its particular category? Note that you will find multiple apps that do the same thing in one category. For example, Games is far and away the most popular category in the Apple app store followed by Education, Entertainment, and Lifestyle. These categories are chocked full of apps with more being designed, developed, approved, and released every day. Your app will really need to stand out if it's targeting one of these categories.

As you go through the lists of popular apps, be sure to navigate to each app's page in the app store. Note the icon for the app; the app's name; its description; screenshots; and last, but not least, the number of reviews and average rating. Most apps listed in the New and Noteworthy section of the App store have impressive download numbers, reviews, and high ratings. Reviews and ratings are important statistics for any app. They are visibly shown on your app's page in the app store, so naturally, you want your app to be popular and well designed in order to receive high ratings from its users.

When reviewing an app's page you will see that screenshots are required for all apps. Take a look at the screenshots for the more popular apps. Note the ones that stand out for you. Note that based on the screenshots, you might be able to get a sense of functionality. That is not the purpose of this exercise. Use the screenshots to get a sense of the design aesthetic of each app. What is unique about the UI of the app? Note the color scheme and what works based on what you can see from the page. Do any of these things make you more or less inclined to download the app? Note why or why not.

Pay special attention to the apps that are in the same category as the app you would like to create. Are there similarities? What clues can you glean from the app's page in the app store about functionality and design?

Every app in the app store will have reviews. Every customer is able to post a public review and rating to the app's page in the app store that everyone will be able to read. Be sure to read the first 10 or so reviews of the top apps in your category as well as those of the apps that appeal to you. Try to get a sense of each reviewer's main concerns. Are they praising the app? Are they trashing it? Reviewers can sometimes be brutally honest, but hidden in some of the most brutal comments are nuggets of truth. So, if users are passionate enough to write a review, there must be some valid points somewhere. If you have downloaded the apps (of course do what your budget allows), then be sure to use the apps and read some of the best and worst reviews to get a balance sense of what the issues in the app are. Compare these to your app. Try to ascertain if your app can fill the void created by some of these applications, especially ones in your category. Make a note of these as well.

You may also want to try app review sites. These are sites that review apps and rate them outside of the app store system. The quality of what you find here might vary but you might also find apps that you don't find in the app store. The difficulty of searching Apple's app store have been debated but is good to get a sense of what Apple deems to be a great example of app design.

Step Four: Analyze your findings

This is the part of the project where we collate all of the data we've collected from the app store and from our own.

Make two lists. One list will contain your favorite apps from your recent app store exploration. Why were you drawn to these particular apps? Describe what stood out to you about these apps. What is unique about them? Was it their names, logo designs, or screenshots? Are there any apps that are similar to your idea? Do any of the apps fall into the same category as your app? Pay special attention to those. Are there lots of similarities between your app and other popular apps? If so, how can you differentiate between yours and theirs? If you need to, revisit your sentence describing your app to think about how your app will be different and how not to reinvent the wheel.

List One:

- App #1 – Great design
- App #2 – Silly name. Has nothing to do with what it does
- App #3 – Love the color scheme

The second list will contain the apps that are specifically from the same category as your idea app. What are the top apps in that category? What are these apps doing right and what are they doing wrong in your opinion? Pay close attention to apps with high ratings and downloads. What are users saying about them and note anything that stands out as unique, positive or negative about these applications. Note anything else about your category. Are most of the apps in your category paid apps or free apps? Is there any consistency among the top rated apps with the best reviews and highest downloads? When you look at the screenshots do you see any similarities in the UI of these apps? What do they do well?

List Two:

- App #1 – Very similar to my app. Reviews complain about price point.
- App #2 – Easy to use. Very popular. Number1 app in the category.
- App #3 – Recommended by Apple. Great design and UI. Easy to use.

Take, for instance, the Utilities category. This category contains many apps with similar functionality. The To-Do apps are a perfect example of this. There are quite a few of these applications in the in the app store, and they all have a similar goal: to help users manage their time or projects by allowing them to categorize their tasks and by creating lists. Each app, however, treats the problem in a different way and while the core task of each application may be the same, each application is markedly different from the other. Each differs in terms of UI, functionality, and color palette. These things alone can make two apps that do similar tasks appear completely different. Think about this in relation to your app and what will make it stand out in a field that just might be already saturated.

An already saturated field isn't a reason to abandon your idea. After all, with almost a million apps in the app store, you'd be hard pressed to find a field that isn't already saturated. So, rather than seeing a potentially saturated category as a barrier to success, think of a saturated field as something that could push you to find a unique way to solve a very popular problem. It will force you to think outside the box and to create a truly original solution to an existing problem.

Step Five: Store comparative apps for future reference

If you can, download as many of the apps on your lists as possible. Hopefully, most of them are free and the others aren't too expensive. Usually apps in the app store range from free to $3.99, but there are others that can be more expensive. Download what your budget allows. Apps costing more than $3.00 or so are considered premium apps and it is up to you to decide what you can afford.

If you choose not to buy apps, try to find reviews of those apps on the Internet. If an app is featured in the App store, then it is likely that it has been featured in popular tech journals like *Mashable*, *Tech Crunch*, or *Venture Beat*. The articles will sometimes go into greater detail about the user interface and functionality of the apps than the description in the app store. A quick Google search should yield a good selection of reviews of some of the top apps. This can save you some cash if you're hesitant to download an app that you won't likely use or one that is not compatible with your budget.

Once the apps have been downloaded, place them in a folder with a title like "Research" or another title that will remind you of its purpose. If you need to, you can further categorize the apps in folders marked paid, free, etc. Keep the folders handy on your phone where you can easily access them if you need to. Throughout this process you will be referring back to these applications to help you with your ideation process.

Step Six: Revise your idea if needed

Once you've downloaded the apps and categorized them, the real fun begins. Keeping your one-sentence description of your app handy (or you should have memorized all of the various versions by now) explore the apps you've downloaded in greater depth. Initially, plan to spend at least a half an hour with each app. You will find that depending on what the app does well, you may spend less or more time with each one. Note this, too. Other questions you might consider asking yourself are:

- What do these apps do well?
- Where do they drop the ball?
- What are the unique elements of their UI?
- Are they easy to use?

More importantly, how do they relate to the app you would like to create?

Pay particular attention to apps that are in the same category as your idea app. How do they compare to the core problem that your application is trying to solve?

If, in our opinion, your app stacks up against these apps then, that is great. You could truly be onto something! If you believe enough in your app, then go for it. While based on the number of apps submitted to the app store each day the numbers alone could stack the odds against you. So, it is important to stand out in any way that you possibly can. Now that you have an idea that you truly believe in, the hard work really begins. Ask yourself the following questions:

- What problem am I trying to solve with my application?
- Who is the intended audience for my application?
- What is the ultimate goal of the application?
- Will the app be available for both the iPhone and iPad?

Once you've answered these questions and none of the answers are showstoppers, then you're ready to proceed with your app. This means that your idea is solid, you've done the basic validation and market research, and you're ready to move onto the next stage of designing your application for iOS.

Summary

All apps start with an idea. But research is critical to your design, too. Creating a statement of what the app does and validating it with others will help you to refine your idea so that it becomes more than just an idea. Checking your app idea against others in the app store is a great way to see what you're up against, get ideas, and understand what users really want. Going through the necessary define and refine process is an important step in the creation of your app and will lay the foundation for the subsequent steps. Next, we'll discuss what you will need to understand about Apple's new operating system, iOS7.

iOS: What You Need to Know

iOS stands for the iPhone Operating System and is the software upon which all of Apple's mobile devices and tablets are built. This includes the iPhone, all versions of the iPad, and even the iPod Touch. iOS allows all of the apps to run on these devices. iOS was released in 2007 with the original iPhone and has undergone minor changes up until recently with the announcement and release of iOS 7.

It is an operating system for multi-touch devices. As such, users are meant to interact directly with the screen of the device upon which the OS is running. This presents some unique opportunities and problems for designers. Therefore, it is important to know what elements are standard and have become familiar to users over the years when interacting with iOS.

Throughout iOS, there are commonly used UI elements that are standard regardless of the device and that help users to perform common actions, regardless of which app is in use. We will review some of these elements, as they will be useful when you design your application.

In June 2013 at the annual Developer's Conference in San Francisco, Apple announced iOS 7. In this chapter, we will discuss standard UI elements for iOS and how they have evolved and changed with iOS 7.

What to Expect in iOS 7

iOS 7 is important because it represents the most significant change in the operating system since its release over six years ago. If you are designing an app from scratch, you will need to understand how Apple expects you to conform to its new design language; and if you already have designed an app, it will need to be redesigned to conform to the new, improved design paradigm set forth in iOS 7.

While the overall functionality of the toolbars, tab bars, navigation bars, and other user interface elements have remained the same, the look and feel of the entire operating system has been changed completely.

As a design-centric company, Apple has always been known for its beautiful, yet simple design aesthetic with its software as well as its hardware. That design aesthetic has become a part of the company's legacy. iOS 7 is an extension of that design aesthetic. While it does not represent a new design paradigm per se (it has borrowed generously in design and has taken hints and clues from some of the more popular apps currently on the market), it does represent a completely new direction for the operating system and will change the way that designers approach the design for their applications moving forward. It is safe to say that applications exhibiting pre-iOS 7 standards will look dated when running on the new OS.

iOS 7 Guiding Principles

Jonathan Ive, Apple's Creative Tsar as he is sometimes called, has always been known for allowing form and function to coexist in a beautiful and seamless way whether it applies to hardware or software, and iOS 7 is no different. Thus, the new interface prides itself on being unobtrusive. Throughout the new updated Human Interface Guidelines (HIG), Apple implores designers to allow the design to facilitate the content. iOS 7 is an attempt to show by doing. Designers who follow in suit will find that their apps look and work seamlessly within the iOS 7 framework.

The key to designing for iOS 7 is to keep it simple. This has always been mentioned in the HIG, but with this new design direction, simplicity is front and center. Older app designs that worked well for the previous version of the OS will now appear heavy and complicated on iOS 7. So, you will have to consider how to adapt to this new color palette while keeping content front and center. While previous upgrades to iOS were focused on development, there are plenty here, too. Designers will be forced to make significant changes in the way that they approach app designs moving forward. All apps must now be optimized for retina screens, and icons have a new look and feel.

There are three guiding principles and themes that should guide designs for iOS 7 apps:

> Deference – Refers to the ability of the user interface to understand and interact with the content of your application but not to compete with it. In fact, the HIG states that the UI should *never* compete with content. This means that the elements you choose in your UI must not overwhelm the content or make the user have to choose between the two. If there is ever any question, content wins. Every time.

> Clarity – Refers to the new requirement that all new designs be legible on retina screens. Previously, if your designs were not optimized for retina screens, they would appear slightly fuzzy on the newer devices. No more. With iOS 7, Apple now requires text and icons to be clear, crisp, and lucid on all devices. That also means no more bevels and drop shadows for effect.

> Depth – New attention has been placed on layers, transparency, translucency, and motion to create depth in applications. iOS 7 is brimming with beautiful transitions and realistic animations that add new responsiveness and depth to the environment.

If you are adapting an older app for iOS 7, you will need to revisit every page to remove the appearance of heavy shadows, bevels, and other features that tend to weight designs down. Remember, functionality and content must be front and center. iOS 7 will expose your app to your users in a whole new way, so think about how you would like to approach a scaled-down look of your app, yet with a heightened functionality in an elegant and stylish way. All of these elements must balance each other out to work with iOS 7.

Now, let's look at a few of the specific changes you can expect with iOS 7. There have been many updates from a development standpoint, but for the purposes of this book, we will focus mainly on those changes that will affect app design moving forward: the springboard, typography, icons, bars, table views, and table view elements.

Springboard

The springboard is where your app icons live on an iPhone or iPad. Everything sits on the springboard. Think of it like your computer's desktop. Upon launching iOS you are presented by and will continually return to the springboard. You will immediately notice the changes to the springboard in iOS 7. Favorite app icons that previously sat at the bottom of the screen on a shiny, beveled shelf, as shown in Figure 2-1, now sit against a translucent background that only partially obscures the wallpaper image as you can see in Figure 2-2. Opening an app now triggers a smoother transition than before, and new settings allow users to set a panoramic image as wallpaper. Moving the phone left or right will produce a "panning motion effect," too. iOS 7 is allowing users to interact with the UI in new ways, and this extends to apps as well. Users are now able to access some settings from the home screen, conduct a spotlight search from the springboard, and swipe down from the home menu to view the new notifications center. I'll go into more detail on how the stock apps have been upgraded for iOS 7 later in this chapter.

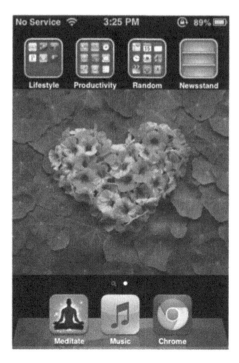

Figure 2-1. Springboard iOS 6 and icons. Favorite apps sit on a shiny shelf

Figure 2-2. Messages and Phone icons now sit in a translucent bar at the bottom of the screen in iOS 7

Typography

The initial release of iOS 7 as well as subsequent releases featured a very skinny Helvetica Neue Ultra Light typeface throughout. It represented a totally different approach and offered a newer, lighter, and more modern look to the operating system. However, it also was difficult to view and thus read in some instances. The most recent release featured a removal from the ultra-light typeface to a heavier, more legible weight. And under the hood, there is a new rendering engine for fonts that allow developers to choose precisely how fonts are to appear throughout their apps. This will provide lots of customization options for designers in the way of typography.

> **Note**   Designers with apps that use heavy text throughout will have to be redesigned for iOS 7.

Something as simple as the text or typeface you choose for your app will become even more important in iOS 7 as it has been noted that new APIs will allow users to use Dynamic Type to adjust the size of text in each app. This puts an additional layer of responsibility on designers when thinking about how their apps will appear to users.

Icons

All of the icons for all standard apps have been redesigned. Gone are the beveled, shadow, and glossy skeumorphic look of the old icons from the previous versions of the operating system. Those of you with a keen eye will remember that as a standard, the old app icons could be used with or without the added sheen and gradient effect that was added programmatically. These effects have been removed altogether and have been replaced with icons that feature a new color palette and an also a new flat look that many of the newer more popular apps now feature. See Figure 2-3 to understand how icons for all stock apps have been reimagined for iOS 7.

Figure 2-3. *iOS 6 & iOS 7 icons side by side*

> **Note**   Is it possible for your creative dept to recreate the chart above? The new iOS 7 icon for Safari is a circle on a white square. Hard to see on image above. Is it possible for the production dept to reproduce this?

It is not only the icons for the stock apps that were redesigned. A quick look at the new Control Center that is accessible with a quick swipe from any page on the springboard will reveal that the icons here have been redesigned in the flat style of iOS 7 as well. These aren't customizable and shouldn't relate to your app, but a quick study is required to fully understand the scope of the changes that iOS 7 brings to the iPhone and iPad.

But, the icons are just the beginning of how Apple has revised the look of all of their standard apps for the iPhone and iPad.

Figure 2-4 shows locked screen view on iOS 6. Note as well how the status bar appears separate from the rest of the screen and the shadowed and beveled buttons on the passcode typepad. iOS 7 does away with all of this.

Figure 2-4. iOS 6 lock screen with passcode entry

Figure 2-5 shows the locked screen view in iOS 7. Specific items to note here are the new appearance of the buttons on the keypad. They now conform to Apple's new "flat" design and are round as opposed to the square keypad buttons used in iOS 6 and previous versions. Note the use of space and how the keypad becomes the focus of this screen. The functionality – entering your passcode is the main focus and nothing takes away from that experience. The experience in the older version is fragmented, with the individual number of windows taking up a significant amount of space on the screen. The consistent use of the circles that we've become used to as page controllers have been elevated in iOS 7. They are now seen in the status bar as signal strength indicators and on the lockscreen as users enter passcodes for access to their devices.

Figure 2-5. iOS 7 lock screen with passcode entry

Bars

Common UI elements in iOS are bars. They are used for multiple purposes such as to show information about the device, to provide a user with additional options or controls, and to display buttons.

Bars vary in size depending on the device but mostly are a constant feature in iOS and are helpful to display critical information to the user. In iOS, they have specifically designed appearances and behaviors in all IOS apps. I've listed the most common bars for iOS below as well as how they've changed with iOS 7.

Status Bar

The status bar provides the user with information about the device such as time of day, battery charge information and networking connection details, and whether an application is accessing a user's location information (Figure 2-6). It sits at the very top of the screen regardless of whether the device is in portrait or landscape mode. When designing your app, there are guidelines for how to use the status bar depending on the look and color palette of your app, and there are a few options you can choose from. Apple does allow you to hide the status bar when a user is viewing key information or playing a game. Other restrictions apply, however, such as using the network indicator to display when an app is utilizing considerable network resources.

Figure 2-6. *The status bar in iOS 7*

Visually some customization of the status bar was allowed but was limited to color and animation. Even though the height of the status bar is fixed, the information that it contains is critical, so if you do decide to hide the status bar, you should be sure that users are not required to quit the application to view it again.

In iOS 7, the status bar has a new updated look and is translucent, transparent, and borderless. Designers will notice that there is no longer a demarcation line that separates the status bar and the navigation bar. Indeed, in iOS 7, they seem to blend into one another. When viewing older apps in iOS 7, the demarcation line still exists, but on every redesigned stock app that ships with an iOS device, it has been removed in favor of Apple's new, simpler UI. You will need to bear this in mind if your application has a colorful background and how the status bar will display on it.

Standard information provided on the status bar includes:

■ Screen orientation – Tells you whether or not your device has been locked in portrait or landscape mode. If your screen hasn't been locked in a particular orientation, you will not see this icon.

■ Cell network's signal or strength – Previously, this information was displayed using bars. In iOS 7, the bars have been replaced by the round indicators.

■ Carrier name – Any of the carriers, including AT&T, Sprint, Verizon, or any of the others.

■ Connection type – 3G, 4G, or LTE are common ones.

■ WiFi Indicator – Lets you know that your device is connected to an available WiFi source and the strength of the signal. Usually one to three bars.

■ Bluetooth – A device using Bluetooth is connected.

■ Time – Displays time of day, usually in the center.

■ Battery indicator – Shows the remaining battery life of the device.

Navigation Bar

The navigation bar allows users to navigate in iOS. It always sits just below the status bar and contains a few key elements. They include the title of the current screen as well as any navigational buttons in the hierarchy of the information on the screen at the given time. The navigation bar will change height and width when a user switches the orientation of his or her device on either the iPad or the iPhone from portrait to landscape.

The look of the navigation bar as well as the elements included on it can be customized. Elements such as the back button, title, and background can all be customized to better align visually with the look and feel of your application.

Apple is specific about **not** creating a multisegment back button or breadcrumb in the navigation bar. There are a few reasons for this. First, it will make the required back button area too large and will infringe on the size of the title of the current screen. Second, listing multiple segments in the back button will decrease the amount of space available for each one, thus making the region available for the user to tap increasingly smaller. And last, the more levels there are, the more it becomes increasingly difficult to decide which levels to display. These are important things to remember, as there is limited real estate on the iPhone and iPod touch.

Much like the status bar, the navigation bar has a new look in iOS 7 (Figure 2-7). It is also translucent and now features borderless buttons. That is to say, there are no buttons at all in the revised navigation bar. Designers should keep in mind what this means in light of the new typography engine in iOS 7 as well. If necessary, work closely with your developer to ensure that your fonts are showing clearly and as you intended in the navigation bar as this governs how users will move through and interact with your application.

Figure 2-7. Navigation bar for Mail app in iOS 7

Toolbar

The toolbar allows users to perform specific actions depending on what a user is seeing in the current view or screen (Figure 2-8). It sits at the bottom of the screen on an iPhone but can be elsewhere on the iPad such as at the top edge of the page. For your toolbar, Apple recommends using the system-provided buttons and icons in your application. However, if your app features custom tasks, then you will need to provide custom buttons and icons for your toolbar. Remember to keep the icons on the toolbar contextual with only the actions relevant to what's taking place on the screen.

Figure 2-8. Common toolbar icons for iOS 7 from the Mail app

On the iPhone, the toolbar will change height with rotation from portrait to landscape so any custom icons will need to be designed to make this adjustment as well.

There are standard icons recommended for use in the toolbar and navigation bars as well. Standard icons for the toolbar are the Flag, Folder, Trash or Recycling, Forward or Share, and Compose.

Tab Bar

Within every application, there will be various custom views and modes that the user will need to navigation among. The tab bar facilitates these actions. It is located at the bottom of the screen and remains consistent. It should be accessible from every location in the app. The default background color for the tab bar was black, but this could be customized depending on your app's design. Now with iOS 7, the tab bar's default color is white and shares many of the same attributes as the navigation bar. There are ways to change the background of the tab bar programmatically, however. There are limits to the tab bar, too. For instance, on the iPhone, no more than five tabs may be displayed at a time in any tab bar. If there are more to show, iOS will automatically add a "More" tab and display the remaining tabs in a list. On the iPad, however, more than five tabs are allowed. The tab bar is consistent regardless of orientation on any device.

You can use the tab bar to communicate information to your user by adding badges, number, and symbols. These will call attention to the tab bar in a way that is not obtrusive to the user and allow easy access when it's convenient for them.

Table Views and Table View Elements

Table views are iOS's unique way of displaying information in a clean and efficient way. They represent one of the most commonly used components of the UI kit for iOS and traditionally appear as a single column list containing multiple rows. These rows can then be divided and separated into groups depending on personal taste and the information being provided for the user. There are two types of table views: A plain table view is one that extends the entire width of the screen. A grouped table view is inset from the background, side, and edges of the screen.

In iOS 7, all table views extend to the edges of the screen. This holds for grouped tables as well that are no longer inset from the background. See examples below in Figures 2-9 and 2-10.

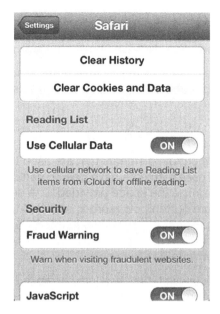

Figure 2-9. *Settings screen in iOS 6 shows a grouped table view*

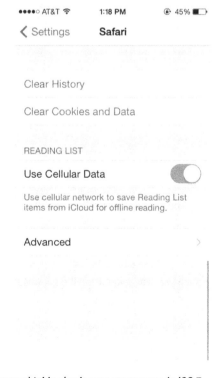

Figure 2-10. *The settings screen and grouped table view's new appearance in iOS 7*

Figure 2-9 above shows the old version of a table view in the settings for the browser app Safari. Note in the old version how the grouped table view is used to set information away from the background and to combine related tasks. Now see how that view has changed in iOS 7.

In Figure 2-10 above, which shows iOS 7 running on an iPhone 5, note the dimensions of the screen are different, and so are the new appearance of grouped table views.

Table View Elements

When interacting with iOS there are certain elements that are used to convey information in various views and situations for the user. These elements have been created to extend the functionality of table views and also help to maximize the space provided. The elements are the checkmark, disclosure indicator, detail disclosure button, row reorder, row insert, delete button control, and the delete button. When designing your app, you will undoubtedly use a table view to display information. While these elements can be used outside of table views in special instances, it is a good rule of thumb to use them within table views only.

Elements that are recommended for use in table views are shown in Figure 2-11. While the tasks associated with these elements remain the same, these elements have also been redesigned for iOS 7.

Element	Name	Description
✓	Checkmark	Indicates that the row is selected
>	Disclosure indicator	Displays another table associated with the row
◉	Detail Disclosure button	Displays additional details about the row in a new view (for information on how to use this element outside of a table, see "Detail Disclosure Button")
☰	Row reorder	Indicates that the row can be dragged to another location in the table
⊕	Row insert	Adds a new row to the table
⊖	Delete button control	In an editing context, reveals and hides the Delete button for a row
Delete	Delete button	Deletes the row

Figure 2-11. This chart from the HIG shows elements commonly used in table views

Note   I'd like to create a chart showing how these elements have changed. Old on the left and new on the right. Can the graphics team recreate this chart it was taken from the hig document by Apple.

Stock Apps

Before you attempt to design for iOS, it is a good idea to take a look at the stock apps that are a part of the iOS stable of applications. They are, in most cases, the first apps you will interact with and are present on every device running iOS. They are Mail, Messages, Calendar, Photos, Camera, Weather, Clock, Maps, Videos, Notes, Reminders, Stocks, Game Center, Newsstand, iTunes, App Store, Passbook, Compass, and Settings. These apps, also shown in Figure 2-12, will help to show you basic design and UI principles for designing applications for iOS. By studying these applications, you will find best practices for using UI elements for common actions in iOS that you can also utilize in your apps.

Figure 2-12. Stock apps in iOS 7

Let's look at a few and call out specific UI elements with which you need to become familiar to design your first app for iOS. What's great about the stock apps in iOS is that the UI elements used in these apps represent established best practices that users of all other platforms will recognize as well.

Mail

Mail is the iPhone and iPad's e-mail application. It allows you to send and receive e-mails from your mobile devices. The Mail application features some standard UI elements that are a key part of iOS and can be used in your application as well. If your application allows users to send e-mails, you will be able to use Mail to send e-mails from your app. The Mail app icon is represented by a blue box with a white envelope on the springboard.

Standard Mail Icons

The compose tool is used to compose an e-mail in the Mail app. The app's icon is represented by a blue box with a white envelope inside. You will see that other third party e-mail applications have some variation on this theme as their app's icon as well. If your app is an e-mail app, it is best not to try to reinvent the wheel. Use established design paradigms and icons in the design of your app.

The compose icon is a commonly used icon to denote the ability to create a new document. Once a user taps on this icon, a new window will appear allowing the user to address a new document or e-mail with a cleared field ready for new content by the user. This is a commonly accepted UI paradigm. If your app allows user to compose a new document or e-mail, use this icon.

Calculator

The Calculator app in Figure 2-13 has been redesigned using the new flat style as well. The previously beveled buttons have been replaced with flat ones and the old shiny entry field is gone as well. This app now uses various shades to differentiate between functionalities of different buttons on the keypad. The new calculator is now easily accessible from the Control Center along with the alarm clock. This removes the need to go into settings as before for access.

Figure 2-13. *The newly redesigned Calculator app in iOS 7*

Calendar

The calendar has a new, cleaner look on a stark, white background in iOS 7. It lets you do many of the same tasks you were able to do in the older versions of iOS. iOS 7 now brings, however, the ability to view the entire year at a glance as shown in Figure 2-14. The navigation is a little different, too. Where in iOS 6 the calendar app had a selector for List, Day, and Month, in iOS 7 tapping a date from the month view will bring up the day view, and in order to see a list view of all events past and upcoming, you will need to tap the search icon in the upper right of the screen of the iPhone. It's not the most intuitive and takes some time to get used to.

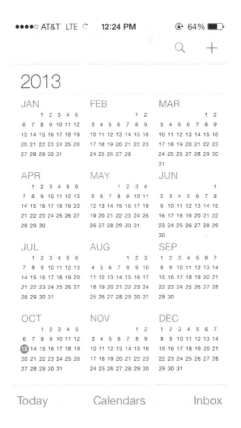

Figure 2-14. The calendar app's new look for iOS 7

Weather

While all of the stock iOS apps have gone through a major transformation, my favorite has to be the Weather app. Not only has the app been redesigned from the ground up, it has added great new animations that do an excellent job of adding context to the overall experience of the app. Here, Apple does a nice job of showing designers how to use the entire screen, something they now implore designers to do. The animations mirror not only the current weather but the current time in the city of your choosing. Front and center is the current city, weather conditions, and temperature. Below, additional information like an hourly breakdown of the weather and temperature is displayed in row and columns evenly spaced for easy reading and visibility (see Figure 2-15). Lower still, is the daily forecast with temperatures for the following five days. The use of space here is balanced, and the subtle background animations are a nice touch especially as they seem to simply float off the screen at the top and sides.

Figure 2-15. *The newly redesigned Weather app*

It is important to note that the Weather app mainly displays information and there is minimal focus on functionality. There are two views: the multicity table view and the one-city view. Users can swipe left or right through the cities on their list or add and delete cities. The interface of the weather app is simple with its content and functionality but somehow, it all works.

Much has also been made of the Weather app's similarity to Yahoo's own weather app. Indeed, the information in the Weather app is drawn from Yahoo and the Weather Channel. Icons and links to both appear in the Weather app. The comparison between the two apps is warranted and definitely worth a look.

Tip   Weather apps have become some of the most popular apps in the Apple app store, and if your app will offer users the opportunity to view weather information, an examination of these apps could help to inform your design.

Color, Transparency, & Layers

As of late, some of the newer and more popular apps have moved away from darker, heavier colors and have adopted a lighter, more pastel color scheme. Apple has adopted this trend, too, and the approach has brought a lighter, cleaner feel to the iOS 7. A bright, white background has replaced the gray and pinstriped background previously found in stock apps like Settings. Now, in Settings, the icons stand out on the clean background. Designers should pay special attention to how Apple uses color, contrast, and transparency to enhance the feeling of depth and to call the user's attention to not only content but context. You can refer back to Figures 2-9 and 2-10 for examples of this.

Using Color

When designing your app, think about how color will play a part in the user interface and help you to tell the story of your app. Every app must have a story and your user interface will help you to tell that story. Colors should complement each other. In iOS 7, Apple sticks to a very clear and specific color palette. You will see the same colors over and over again in use throughout all of the stock applications. Pay special attention to how and where they are used. For instance, the almost fluorescent green used in the Messages app is used in the battery bar indicator in the status bar and in the phone app icon. That same green is used as an accent color in the Passbook and Contacts icons as well. Think about the use of color in specific areas and about associating color with specific tasks as well.

Users will begin to understand the importance of color more than ever with iOS 7. For instance, a user's background image or wallpaper will affect the look of the entire way the UI renders. If your wallpaper or background has yellow as the main hue, this color will present itself on the lock screen keypad, and the transparency of the folders on the springboard will allow the dominant color to seep through, thus giving the device properties of that color and casting it in that light. It's a nice, subtle touch that allows an added layer of customization so that no two devices will look exactly the same when running iOS 7.

Using Transparency

Transparency and translucency are other tools used generously, yet subtly in iOS 7. In addition to the aforementioned folders on the springboard, an upward swipe from any page will reveal the new Control Center. It's an easy way to access some of your most commonly used apps and provides a shortcut to controls without navigating to the Settings app that some people (myself included) tend to hide or tuck way in a folder. First, the Control Center's panel is translucent and really brings to life the three-dimensional quality of the operating system, something that was missing from previous versions. Not only does it reveal that there is a layer of applications and other functionality underneath, it lets their colors shine through. The panel appears as a thin pane of glass over the springboard itself. See Figure 2-16 for an example of the Control Center panel over the home screen. Second, the Control Center's panel doesn't extend to the top of the screen. On the iPhone, it reveals one and a half rows of apps and folders on the springboard. This offer users context as to where they are in the OS. They are free to navigate away in two ways: swipe down on the panel itself; or simply tap another icon, and the panel removes itself. The approach is simple, yet incredibly effective.

Figure 2-16. *The translucent bar of the Control Center. The Control Center will show the color of the page underneath: in this case, the wallpaper*

Designers should reference these subtle clues when designing their apps and when deciding how users are meant to interact with the content in their apps, too. This iteration of the operating system pushes designers to strip away elements that are not absolutely necessary and to focus on elements those users will need to interact with your application.

Using Layers

Layers are a key component of iOS 7. Whereas in previous versions the focus was on adding effects like bevels and shadows to infer and imply depth, iOS 7 has organized everything in layers and used motion sensors to offer users a three-dimensional feel while using their device. Thus, as users move, the layers also move and complement the users' views. So, the element currently in use is always on the foremost layer. This means that content behind it will shift and recede where necessary to offer this illusion of depth and space between all of the elements in front of you. Even the act of opening an app shows depth. The older version of the OS offered users a quick zoom when opening apps; in iOS 7, the opening screen of the app still zooms inward but the background seems to shift back as well, creating a feeling of total immersion in the new app.

Buttons

The borders that were standard in previous versions of the iOS have mostly been removed. This could present an issue because users will now have to relearn spatially where the tappable space is around a word. Users have come to expect a border around buttons like "Back" and "Cancel." Because of their familiarity with iOS, users will instinctively know what these buttons do (their names also give it away). Various versions of iOS 7 had just flat colorful bars where there once were buttons. The End Call and Call buttons in the phone app have evolved in recent beta versions of iOS 7 from borderless but colorful bars to proper buttons with outlines.

Summary

With all of the sweeping changes to iOS; a complete overhaul rolling out over new devices, the future of design for iOS applications is bright. As a leader in design, Apple has established some long-standing design standards and borrowed from others. They are now poised to change things again. By setting new standards, designers will now be forced to come up with newer and exciting ways to visually communicate with users via their apps.

What remains interesting is where the iOS 7 will push the direction of design. Admittedly, the changes that Apple has made to iOS can be traced back to other platforms (Android and Windows Phone to name two). But design aficionados have always seen Apple as a leader in this field. When designing your app, think about not just this new version but where it's come from and its evolution. Ask yourself what the next big step is, and then take it.

iOS 7 and Flat Design

As you prepare to design your app and as you have begun to familiarize yourself with all of the principles of the Human Interface Guidelines and iOS 7, you undoubtedly have heard the phrase "Flat Design" bandied about. It is a term being used to define Apple's new direction to the user interface of the operating system. So, it's only fair to define flat design and to explain not only what it is and where it comes from, but also how you can use it to create your very own app. As you set out to create your app, think about the content and bringing that front and center. One thing to remember is that users have now been interacting with multi-touch and Apple's suite of mobile devices for some time now.

We've reviewed the sections of the Human Interface Guidelines that were specifically updated to provide guidance on iOS 7. You should be familiar with them by now. There are very specific expectations with regard to the placement of specific elements in the UI, many of which were defined by the Human Interface Guidelines. Luckily, iOS 7 does not change the placement of those elements, but the look and appearance of the elements are markedly different. Once iOS 7 is widely released (it will be by the time this book has been published), users will have become reconditioned to the way that these elements appear.

In this chapter, we will take a deeper dive in the flat design, how it came about and what you need to know when designing your iOS application.

The Principles of Flat Design

Flat design represents a sort of minimalism that moves away from the realism of skeuomorphism. Though simpler to look at, it is seen as being more sophisticated and versatile than its realistic cousin skeuomorphism. Flat design also offers more clean lines and a lighter, bolder, and more colorful palette of colors to attract viewers and to provoke emotion.

Some design purists say that utilizing flat design principles is a way to elevate content and letting functionality take center stage. This means to me, that it becomes more critical for designers to either work closer with UI and UX or to have a better understanding of these principles. Previously, designers were the guys who came into make wireframes pretty. Now, with flat design the designer and UX could very well be the same person. Without the old visual cues to guide users, buttons and other UI elements need to be more intuitive. The only things to guide users aside from visual feedback will now be their own knowledge and understanding of what feels natural and makes sense. This new way of designing moves the overall user experience to the forefront of the entire design process. Indeed, with the stripping away of many of the extraneous elements and effects like bevels and shadow, the user comes face-to-face with the experience and the content. Your job as designer is to make sure that it stands up.

The Origin of and Other Uses of Flat Design

Outside of iOS 7, you will find plenty of other examples of flat design. Apple did not invent flat design and even though we are speaking of it in terms of iOS, it is not a mobile-specific paradigm, either. You will be able to find multiple examples on the Web as well as in other mobile operating systems (Windows Phone and Android are a few) and in countless apps whose designs were exhibiting flat design principles before Apple took notice.

The unlikely hero behind bringing flat design to the forefront is none other than Microsoft. And it did it with a little-known and now-extinct music player called Zune. Although Zune never really made a dent in iTunes's virtual domination of the music software industry, what it did do was to set the stage for a new design sensibility that Microsoft and other software companies would use moving forward. Soon, others followed the flat design trend.

Software giant Google also joined the flat design trend before Apple to represent all of its properties, logos, and icons. The official Google Visual Assets Guidelines uses flat design principles liberally throughout.

Even popular consumer brands have embraced the flat design trend. A look at popular brands like eBay, the aforementioned Microsoft, and even Twitter, have recently embraced flat design principles in reimagining their logos and branding.

eBay notably changed its logo in 2012 for the first time in its 17-year history to reveal a newer and, yes, flatter design. While the company has not formally mentioned flat design in the language announcing the change, the principles are clear for anyone who dares to compare the two logos. The branding and colors remain intact; however, what is difficult to miss are the use of a thinner font and the removal of the overlapping of letters in the company name. Some would argue that the colors are already flat design friendly and the skinny font only adds to the flat effect.

Following the flat design trend, as well, was Twitter whose popular "Twitter bird" logo was redesigned for the first time in the microblogging company's six-year history. In a note on the site's official blog, creative director Doug Bowman speaks of the new design direction as being born out of a love of "design within creative constraints and simple geometry." He goes on to state that the bird is "crafted purely from three sets of overlapping circles." Those of you familiar with the magic grid system used to create the design for Apple's new icons can see lots of similarities there.

> **Tip**   Examine and review how big brands have adapted to the flat design trend. Use them as examples when designing your app.

The Future of Flat Design

The design community has been buzzing about the flat design trend for some time now. Some tend to think it is just a trend and others think it's here to stay. However, a June 2013 survey of web professionals across a number of different design professionals conducted by Usabilla, a website usability tool, yielded the following conclusions.

People associate flat design with the following descriptions:

> Simple
>
> Clean
>
> Colorful
>
> Modern
>
> Boring

The five main advantages of flat design are the following:

> Clarity
>
> Ease of use
>
> Modern appearance
>
> Efficient responsive design
>
> Fast load times

The five main disadvantages of flat design are listed here:

> Different from what people are used to
>
> Difficult to execute well
>
> Unclear what's clickable
>
> Boring design
>
> Lack of personality

Based on these lists, flat design is not just a trend. It is here to stay. Sixty-eight percent of respondents believe that flat design isn't just a fad but that it will truly affect the way we design for the Web and mobile for years to come.

Incorporating Flat Design into Your App

So, what do the survey results mean for you and the design of your application? Because flat design principles are here to stay, you will need to incorporate them into the design of your app. Let's look at each of the following principles in more depth.

- Choosing a Color Palette
- Designing Icons
- Utilizing Space and Templates

- Defining Buttons
- Simplifying Forms
- Determining Typography
- Evaluating Usability

Choosing a Color Palette

Understanding that bright bold colors are the hallmarks of flat design, this does not mean you can throw reason out the window when it comes to color. You must choose your colors wisely.

Color is critical to your application so defining a color palette is one of the most important tasks you will undertake when designing your app. The first thing you will need to understand is whether or not there are important branding guidelines that you must be aware of for you or your client. Whether you are designing your app for yourself or for a client, you must be aware of the emotions that certain colors evoke in users. There are a number of online resources that can help designers understand the psychology behind the use of certain colors; so do some research before you choose a palette for your app. Be aware that flat design skews toward bright, bold, and vivid colors to communicate specific messages to users. Refer back to your application documentation and the primary tasks users will be performing in your app to find the right color combination for you. Be sure to experiment as well because the possibilities are endless.

Here are some questions to ask when trying to decide on a color palette:

What color or colors would best highlight the main tasks in your application?

Are you using a range of shades of a specific color? For instance, is your main color scheme a specific shade of red as well as a number of other reddish shades?

What are the roles of neutral colors such as grays, blacks, and whites in your design?

Are the colors you choose complementary? Do they work next to each other on the page?

Whatever you do, your app must be consistent. If your app opens with bright, bold colors, you should stick with this approach throughout. Don't transition to a muted, softer palette later on.

There are a number of great online resources for designers when considering palettes for flat design. One of my favorites is Flatuicolors.com (http://www.flatuicolors.com). It's a simple web app that lists some popular flat UI colors and lets you paste it in a number of different formats (hex, rgb, etc.) You can use it to try out different color combinations in your app.

Another helpful tool is Color Scheme Designer (http://www.colorschemedesigner.com). This is a designer's wonderland that allows you to view and test palettes of various colors. It shows them side-by-side and helps designers to understand how colors look side-by-side and also how they interact and complement each other. It's possible to customize the view by triad, tetrad, and even mono—and the combinations seem virtually endless.

If brash, bold colors aren't your thing, muted, monotone colors work, too. Many popular apps have been experimenting with more muted tones of primary and secondary colors. If anything, try to push the conventional color boundaries with your choice of color schemes.

> **Tip** Try to stay away from color generalizations such as pink to denote feminine and blue for masculine.

Designing Icons

Because of the lack of realism in flat design and the elevation of content, icons and illustrations have become increasingly more important. Icons are used in design to communicate certain messages to the user. They are visual shortcuts that you use in your applications to help users navigate their way through the app.

While there are a number of design resources available online to assist designers with their icons, some designers choose to create their own. Icons can bring an element of personality to your app and contribute to your users' understanding of the UI elements in your app. Think about Apple's icons and how they have evolved with flat design. If you design your own icons, remember that users will already associate certain actions with certain icons in the operating system so there is no need to reinvent the wheel.

When you decide to create your own icons, the following are some guidelines to remember:

- Your icons should be simple and clean.

- Remove extraneous elements that confuse users and stick with only elements that absolutely must be present.

- Icons should be intuitive: that is to say that users should be able to understand the meaning behind an icon by a simple look. If a user must interact with an icon to figure out the intended meaning, then your design has failed its most important task.

- Think about the overall use of the app and its purpose. Are your icons appropriate to the subject matter? Be sure that your icons are appropriate to the task they are trying to convey and to the overall purpose of your app.

- Your icons should always be drawn as clearly and as cleanly as possible. The HIG provides guidelines about how icons will need to be scaled so that they do not appear fuzzy when viewed on retina screens.

- Your icons should appear consistent across a number of different devices with different screen resolutions.

- Flat design usually applies simple shapes for icons. They will either be circles, squares, or rectangles; so if you choose to go with a shape for your icons, then you should stick with that to be consistent. Mixing and matching icon shapes is a sure way to confuse and befuddle your users. It is always a good idea to refer back to iOS icons as a general guide for creating your own as well.

> **Tip** There are also a number of resources for flat design icons on the Internet. There are downloadable icon packs, some of which are free and some that will cost a nominal fee.

Utilizing Space and Templates

When designing for iOS 7 and when considering elements of flat design, the use of space is an important factor. On the Web, flat design principles usually leave lots of empty space in keeping with the "less is more" principle that guides flat design. So, too, in iOS 7, the use of space is important. Although there is less space on mobile devices than there is on desktops, you should think about how the use of space will translate across the different devices that your app will run on.

To get started with your app design for iOS 7, a flat design, there are a number of flat design templates available for free download on the Web. Do a search for "iOS 7 GUI PSD Template" to find one that suits your needs. Templates for the iPhone and iPad are available. These templates include everything you need to get started to at least play around with the UI elements and how they could be used and positioned within your applications. You can use these templates to create your wireframes, too.

You can also find design inspiration on visual sites like Pinterest to see what other designers are doing or, you can take the plunge yourself into the world of flat design. There are some basic elements that will need to change in every application in order for flat design to be fully implemented. We've touched on color space and icons, but let's get more specific.

Defining Buttons

Buttons are an important part of every app's interface. Users are accustomed to buttons being activated to perform a certain function – usually, whatever is written on the label. For instance, the buttons in Figure 3-1 show examples of a regular traditionally designed button on the left and a flat design button on the right. Note the removal of the drop shadow and bevel on the left and the emphasis on simplicity on the right button.

Figure 3-1. Old button with drop shadow vs. new flat style button

The old button clearly shows a three-dimensional quality that is commonplace in skeuomorphism. The new button removes that and replaces the three-dimensional effect with a decidedly two-dimensional one. This is a prime example of how buttons have evolved in the face of flat design. Also note that traditionally designed buttons usually are darker in color and shade, giving them a heavier look and feel.

In iOS 7, while buttons maintain their flat appearance, subtle changes have been made in their appearance to allow for better usability. Note the Phone app interface changes between two different versions of iOS 7 in Figures 3-2 and 3-3:

Figure 3-2. *iOS 7 beta 4. iOS 7 Beta 4's call button extends to the edge of the screen*

Figure 3-3. iOS 7 beta 7. iOS 7 Beta 7's call button now features rounded edges

While both button treatments adhere to flat design principles, the older version from beta 4 features no outline or demarcation to note where the boundaries of the button lie. The newer approach creates an actual button outline and adds rounded corners. I've seen apps that utilize either approach with great results. But, keep in mind that subtle changes such as these can make a world of difference for your users.

Simplifying Forms

Another oft-forgotten UI element that has evolved along with flat design is the form. Mobile apps use forms for sign-ups and sign-ins. Although users are typically not asked to sign in more than once, forms previously included inset shadows to denote depth and space. But, search fields now offer no such enhancements. When designing your forms for sign-in and registration fields, keep your windows clean and devoid of all effects. A thin border outline will usually do the trick, but also try to experiment with different shades of gray or stark white for form backgrounds. Figure 3-4 shows the input form for the iTunes Store. Note the simple field for entry of a user's password.

Figure 3-4. Pop-up windows and notifications and forms have a new look in iOS 7

Determining Typography

Possibly one of the most important elements of flat design is the typography that you will use in your app. Since flat design focuses on typography, you will need to find a font that evokes the overall feeling and message that you would like for your application to convey. Because flat design is simple and minimalist, your font should probably be as well, so choose a maximum of two types of font families for your app. Make sure that the fonts complement each other. If you have any conflicts, it is fine to use just one font throughout your app and experiment with different weights to convey meaning. Fonts and type that feature clean lines and strokes will tend to look better in flat design schemes. Toward this end, san serif typefaces are incredibly popular with designers utilizing flat design techniques in their mobile apps and web apps. I've created a chart with some popular sans serif typefaces in Figure 3-5.

Learn Design for iOS - Helvetica Neue

Learn Design for iOS - Helvetica

Learn Design for iOS - Geneva

Learn Design for iOS - Calibri

Figure 3-5. San serif typefaces are commonly used in flat designs

The colors and weights of your fonts are also important so consider a font that comes in a variety of weights that you will be able to use throughout your app. You may want to consider a specific weight for buttons and icons and use others for call to actions while body text might be a lighter weight.

Evaluating Usability

There have been subtle changes in certain elements of the interface. While still maintaining its flat appearance for user interface elements, they have been finely tuned for usability. Make no mistake: usability is a big part and reason for the transition to flat design. There has been some debate in the design community about just how user friendly flat design is. Some critics contend that for all its beauty and performance enhancements, flat design can, at times, be confusing for users. Sure, the stripping away of the very elements and effects that make buttons seem like, well, actual buttons *can* cause a bit of disorientation for users. iOS 7 does its fair share of removing those elements. Take, for instance, the removal of the tiny dividing lines in the tab bar. Now, those elements at the bottom of this screen, which were clearly delineated, now seem to float in midair. (See Figures 4-6 and 4-7 above.) This is where a designer must use his or her discretion to understand what makes sense from a usability standpoint. It's up to you and your user how these elements are going to be interpreted. Therefore, if you genuinely feel that a small drop shadow will help users to interact better with an element of your app, then by all means find the balance between flat design and realism and add the drop shadow. There is no need to overdo it. With flat design, less is more, and you will find that adding subtle hints of realism in an app that could otherwise be flat design overkill, may strike the perfect balance for your user.

Flat design is challenging because it, in essence, removes all of the elements that help users to associate what is on their screen with what actually exists in the real world. The very metaphors that we use to translate the virtual to the physical are being removed with flat design. Thus, what was a button is now just a flat square on a background. The visual cues we as designers created to reference real-world properties like light and shadows have been removed. So, what's left? Your content and the user. The question then becomes, how can we still provide those cues to users who live in a three-dimensional world but who are interacting within a two-dimensional construct? If you choose to wholeheartedly take a complete flat design approach to your app, you must consider these realities when you think about how users will maneuver within your application.

Apple has allowed for some other ways of merging this new two-dimensional world with the addition of three-dimensional effects like a parallax and the use of transparency. These features, which are already core tenets of the operating system, are a part of the arsenal of tools available to designers to enhance the overall experience and usability of their applications. These effects can help to provide visual cues to users.

Summary

When you consider the overall user experience of your application, you must think strategically. Every decision, then, you are considering your approach to design and just how far down the rabbit hole you need to go, becomes a strategic one. As a designer, your task is to find the delicate balance between what a user sees and what he or she feels. All of this is contained within the world that you create through design within your app. Can flat designs help you to achieve this goal? By this point the purpose of your app and the audience you are attempting to reach should be crystal clear. Undoubtedly, you will have to employ flat design techniques in your app; the question is just how much.

Chapter 4

Getting to Know the User Interface of the iPhone and iPad Design Considerations

Designing for the iPhone and iPad require a clear understanding of the user interface of both devices. There are similarities across both, and there are clear guidelines and documentation to follow these guidelines to ensure that your application adheres to the standards set forth by Apple. Within that however, there is still plenty of room to be creative and unique with your design. While Apple might seem strict in its enforcement of its design guidelines and rules, there is always room to experiment and they encourage it with designs, especially ones that show a clear understanding of the underlying precepts upon which iOS was built.

We addressed the standard UI elements in the previous chapter, so now we will move into how to familiarize yourself with the user interface of the devices. A great way to start to become familiar with the UI is to download one of the freely available GUI kids available for iOS. GUI kits are available for the iPhone and iPad and most of them are free. Teehan & Lax creates a PSD GUI kit for iOS 6 and 7 as does Applidium.

Once you download the GUI in the format of your choice, you will be able to explore the various elements in more detail. Import the file into the graphic software of your choice; this way you can begin to interact with them. Most of them have been created by designers and design shops with the intention of helping the design community so you don't have to reinvent the wheel when starting to design your app.

Once you have your GUI open, take a close look at how they appear compared to the actual device. Most elements will have a selection of bars (status, header, tab, etc.) as well as buttons, action sheets (Figure 4-1), keyboards, and icons. You should be able to view them or even to remove them from the GUI if you need to inspect themmore closely.

Figure 4-1. An action sheet from the stock iOS7 Mail app

> **Note**   An action sheet is a menu in iOS that displays a set of choices for the user. The choices are usually related to a task initiated by the user.An action sheet from the Mail app is shown in Figure 4-1.

Get to know each user interface element and begin to think about how each element will be used in your app.

Which bars will you use?

Will you need to create a custom icon for a status bar in your menu?

Will your app have a unique color scheme?

How will you lay out critical information for your users?

How does each element help the user on his or her journey throughout the app?

Take the time you need to become familiar with the UI; after that, then you can begin to think about how to customize the experience for your users. You don't have to use all of the elements as they appear. You are allowed a fair amount of flexibility and creativity with the UI for your app. But first, it's important to understand the basics before you step outside. This is the purpose of this chapter.

Use of Gestures in the UI

The iOS interface is optimized for a unique multi-touch experience. As such, elements on screen respond to touch, or gestures, and not clicks. It is important, therefore, to always remember that users must feel as though they are engaging directly with content. Your design must engage userswith an immersive experience within your app. What elements will allow them to do that? Users interact with iOS by using specific gestures. These gestures have become commonplace not just within iOS but with other multi-touch platforms and operating systems as well; however,some of them were coined by Apple.

When discussing gestures for iOS, two important concepts to consider are the aforementioned consistency and direct manipulation.

Consistency of Gestures

When considering user interface elements and appropriate gestures for your app, consistency is key. Use gestures that result in actions that are consistent with the established best practices and user expectations. If a user swipes left and expects a panel or content to move in that direction and it moves right instead, you are creating a significant disconnect between the user and the interface. A user then has to spend time understanding which gestures mean what in your app, and this provides a disorienting experience, especially outside of your app when they are interacting with stock iOS apps or other apps that follow established rules.

If your app's interface elements are not consistent with iOS standards or use system-wide controls, views, and icons incorrectly or differently, you should consider changing them. Not doing so may result in your app being rejected from the app store.

Direct Manipulation of Gestures

Direct Manipulation is a concept of gesture control that refers to interacting with an object on a screen as though it were a real object. Thus, tapping a button is like pressing a button in real life. And pulling a lever is akin to pulling a real lever or slider. iOS is based on this principle of gesture control. And it gives users the perception of actually manipulating their controls. These direct manipulation controls proliferate throughout iOS and should now be familiar to users. Actions such as "Slide to unlock" from the home screen and "pull to refresh," which can be seen from the Mail app are now popular in other apps. Users will intuitively perform these actions without instruction and inmany cases will expect them in your application. The reason why these types of gestures are popular with users is because there is a direct and immediate relationship between the action and the result. Users will feel as though they are carrying out the action in real life. Designers and developers should use these gestures in their apps where it is obvious that users will be expecting them. Not using them can frustrate your user base.

Abstract Gestures and Feedback

Abstract commands and gestures are gestures that offer the user very little or no relation between the action and what is shown on the screen. Because these are not immediately intuitive to the user, these gestures will require some level of memorization for your users. If you must use an abstract gesture, make sure that you've tested with a target group to ensure that you are not alienating your audience by introducing gestures that aren't familiar to them. Users will need to memorize the new abstract gestures you introduce with your app and learn to associate them with a specific action if they are to successfully navigate and interact with your application.

iOS does a good job of staying away from abstract gestures altogether, but there are some apps that while not abstract per se, do require a user to memorize new gestures for new actions even though there is a direct relation to what is shown on the screen. The popular e-mail app Mailbox is one such app. Users who have used the stock Mail app will find that they will need to learn new gestures for variousactions. For example, in Mailbox, swiping right lets a user archive a message, but a long swipe to the right will put a message into the trash folder. Swiping left will let a user snooze a message for later, whereas a long swipe left will add the message to a number of lists. The app uses colorful indicators as visual feedback to let users know what action he or she is taking, but the gestures will take some getting used to—especially if a user has been using the standard Mail app. Luckily, the app makers include a helpful tutorial that is easily accessible from the Help section of the app. A view of the Mailbox app and iOS's Mail app are shown in Figure 4-2.

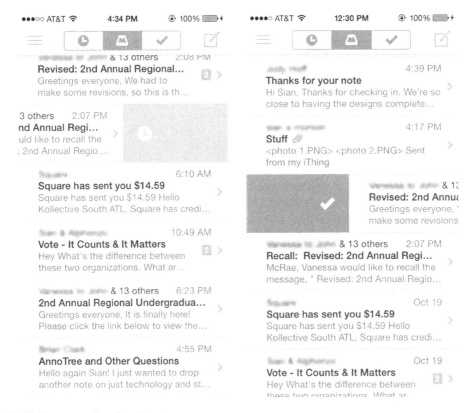

Figure 4-2. The Mailbox app actions for old gestures

Feedback is another interaction principle that is very important in designing user interfaces for iOS. Feedback is a mechanism by which a user's action is acknowledged, and he or she is aware that the intended process or outcome of said action is actually taking place (Figure 4-3). Stock iOS apps all have some element of feedback in them. For instance, pulling down to refresh a list of messages in a table view in the Mail app will reveal a spinner as the app connects with the server to download new messages. Also, initiating the process of updating an app will present a progress bar so that users are aware of the progress of the download. If the action is not successful, the app will let the user know usually by displaying a message of some sort. Sound can also be used as a powerful feedback indicator for any given initiated action. Using the Mail app as another example, a "ding" is the default sound for when new e-mails have been downloaded from the server. While these sounds can be changed in settings, some of themhave become accepted norms for users within iOS.

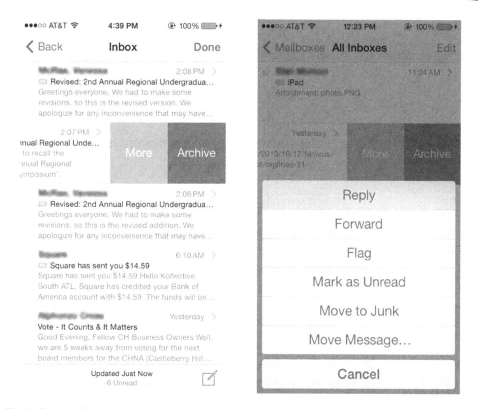

Figure 4-3. The Mail app in iOS7 uses color as a notifier of a specific task

Gestures in iOS

There are a few different types of gestures that all users of iOS devices will find themselves using at some point or another. They are commonplace across all iOS apps and have now become a familiar part of the multi-touch lexicon. These are gestures that will feel "natural" to the user, are easily discoverable, and give the impression that they are interacting directly with the content they see on the screen. They are the following: Tap, Double Tap, Swipe, and Pinch, among others. The gestures listed here are commonplace in iOS and represent accepted paradigms for use in multi-touch devices and application across platforms.

Tap

A tap is the multi-touch equivalent of a click that users perform with a keyboard or a mouse. It allows users to select a control or an item that they see on the screen of their device.

Double Tap

A double tap allows a user to zoom in and center on an image or content. If a user is already zoomed in, then the reverse happens and the action will result in a zoom out.

Drag or Pan

A drag is a movement from side to side with a finger or fingers. The resulting action is a horizontal pan effect.

Flick

A flick is a faster version of a drag. A flick happens when a user moves his or her fingers quickly up or down on the screen.

Swipe

A swipe is an action that usually reveals the delete button in a table view. It is also used to move panels to the left or right depending on the application.

Pinch

A pinch applies using two fingers to create to a zooming view and is used to make an image or content smaller or bigger within a view on the screen. A user can pinch to zoom in or reverse the action to zoom out.

Touch and Hold

In text that is editable such as a message or the contents of a browser window, touch and hold will show a magnified view and allow the user to position the cursor anywhere within the text for easy editing.

Shake

While this isn't a standard gesture or action, the shake initiates an undo or a redo of a previous action. However, innovative app developers have recently used the shake gesture in a variety of ways that have little to do with redo or undo actions.

New iOS Gestures

New releases of iOS have sometimes introduced new gestures, and there have been rumors of new gestures being introduced with iOS7. If you decide to experiment with newer gestures in your application you will need to conduct thorough testing with potential users to ensure that the new gestures are intuitive and that users see desired and expected results by using them. Apple has done a great job with introducing new gestures. Of the rumored new gestures in iOS7, I've confirmed the following:

Swipe Up

This action when performed from any screen reveals the control center. After interacting with the controls on the Control Center screen, users may swipe down to reveal the page underneath. A swipe up is also used to exit or close an active or open app from the multitasking switcher view. This action was not previously associated with this result in older versions of iOS.

Swipe Down

This action from the top edge of any screen reveals the Notification Center that shows all undismissed notifications for the current day as well as those you may have missed. Swiping up closes the notification panel. Swiping down from the home inside the home screen will reveal the spotlight search. Previously, the spotlight search was found by swiping to the right of the first page on the springboard. An example of this is shown in Figure 4-4.

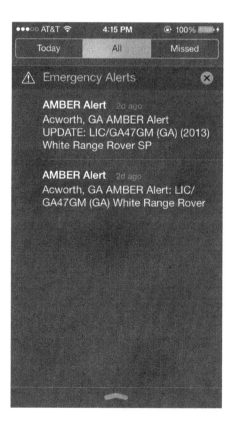

Figure 4-4. The notification bar and Spotlight Search are accessed by the swipe down action

Swipe Right (In Mail App)

Swiping right in the mail app while viewing a message in its entirety (not preview) will take the user back to the list view and previews of all messages in a scrollable table view.

The iPad; How Is It Different?

The iPad was released on April 3, 2010, to mixed reviews and some ridicule and jokes because of its name. It marked Apple's entry into the still relatively new tablet computer field. Today, there are currently a few different types of iPads on the market. The first generation iPad is no longer supported and won't be able to run iOS7. For the purposes of this book, we will focus only on current iPad models still supported by Apple and available for purchase from Apple.

It is easy to think that the iPad is just a larger version of the iPhone. This assumption would be incorrect. The iPad is more a computer than it is a phone, and the way that people interact with the iPad vs. the iPhone is very different. Designers must remember this. It is easy, though, to understand why the iPad is thought of as just an oversized iPhone; it looks almost exactly like an iPhone does. However, the iPhone is an entirely different device than the iPad. Users who use the iPad also often have an iPhone as well, but their expectations are different when using the iPad. As the top-selling tablet ever, the iPad is owned by a large and varied demographic. According to a recent study by the analytics company Flurry, they run the gamut from children, moms, home design enthusiasts, and small business owners. Therefore, as with any other application, your iPad application must be designed with a specific demographic in mind.

E-commerce is also a large part of the iPad market. The iPad dominates the tablet market when it comes to online shopping and traffic generation. With this in mind, it is important to understand not just what people are doing on the iPad but *how*.

The iPad, in terms of the class of device that it is, sits between the phone and the computer; it is also between the iPhone and the Mac and is meant to allow users to do more than they could on an iPhone only. Expectations on what the iPad can do are increasing with each new release. Currently, there are threedifferent iPads on the market. They are the following:

- The iPad Mini: The iPad mini is the most recent addition to the iPad family. It was released in November of 2012 and is a smaller version of the iPad aimed at targeting users who were more inclined toward readers such as the Kindle and Nook.

- The iPad 2: The iPad 2 was released in March of 2011. This version of the iPad is both lighter and thinner than the original, first generation iPad. Unlike the iPad mini and Retina versions of the iPad, the iPad 2 still has the old 30-pin connector. It was also the first iPad to featuredual facing cameras.

- The iPad Retina: This was released in March and October 2012 respectively; the third and fourth generations of the iPad are very similar. The iPad 4 Retina uses the new lightening connector. It also introduced a newer, faster processor for downloading content from the Internet and for processing graphics. The iPad 3 has been discontinued.

Currently, when a designer submits an app for the iPad, it must be tested and shown to perform optimally on all iPads. The iPad with Retina screens have a high pixel count and can make well-designed apps look stunning. Unfortunately, it also highlights the imperfections in bad or low-res designs. It is believed that moving forward, *all* iOS app submissions must include assets for Retina as well as lower res supported devices.

So, what exactly is different about the iPad? Well, for starters, it's larger than the iPhone and allows more real estate for multi-touch interactivity and room for additional design elements. Also, the way that the iPad is used differs from the way users interact with their iPhones. IPhone users are mobile. They are on the go, and they use their devices to help them along their busy lifestyles. iPad users are typically using the device in a classroom, on a couch or in a "lean-back" situation. Consider these things when you think about the design of your iPad application:

How will users hold the device when they are interacting with your app?

Will your app work in both portrait and landscape?

Which orientation suits the tasks associated with your app better?

What are users likely to be doing when they are using your app?

What environments will they be in and how will it affect their use of the device?

These things will all matter when you begin to design your iPad app. The extra real estate that the iPad affords designers should be used wisely. Do not fill it with unnecessary, unneeded elements that don't add value to the user or the overall experience of the app. Add UI elements that enhance the user's understanding of the space and environment that your app has created and in which he or she will be working.

The guidelines that Apple set for designing for the iPad are similar to those for the iPhone; the same principles regarding content, usability and context will still apply. Figure out what functionality is absolutely needed and provide that for your users. Use personas to think about who your users are and how each persona will interact with the app. It is possible that each persona will have different needs. Make sure that what's needed is easily accessible at all times. If users have to try to find something that they feel should be obvious, it leads to a bad user experience, and potentially bad review.

> **Note**   A persona is a fictional character that represents a subset of users with a specific group of characteristics and behaviors when interacting with your app. Personas are helpful in validating design and user experience.

Although most of the navigational items are the same, the iPad does have a few UI elements that are not available for the iPhone, such as the popover and the split view screen.

Popover View

A popover is a view that presents itself over the contents of an existing screen. It usually will have a point or arrow of some sort to orient the user to where it has emerged and should cover whatever is behind it so that the user is able to focus on the content within it. Many different types of information and UI elements can be placed within a popover. It can contain a table view with a list, additional options for the user displayed in an action sheet, or contents of a left pane in a split view. Apple lays out specific instructions on how to use a popover so be sure to read the Human Interface Guidelines to get instructions on its usage.

While it is permissible to use standard UI controls within popovers, it is never ok to add a "Close" or "Dismiss" button. Dismissing a popover should follow the existing iOS paradigm, which is to disappear whenever a user taps anywhere outside of it or anywhere else on the screen. The close or dismiss button is a common web paradigm that does not exist in iOS. Also while there is no height restriction, there is a width restriction of 320–600 points. This can depend on the information being displayed on your design. Figure 4-5 shows popovers with two different lengths.

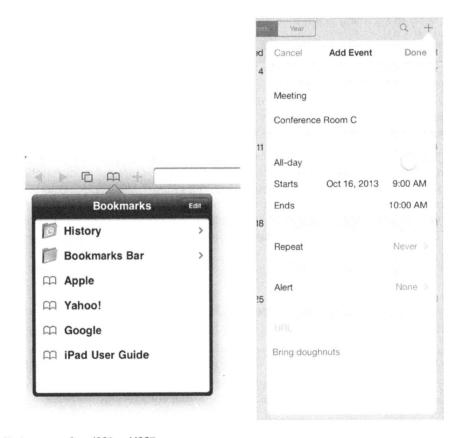

Figure 4-5.   iPad popovers from iOS6 and iOS7

It is permissible to find clever and novel ways so show your popovers. Think out of the box but always keep the user experience front and center.

Split View Screen

A split view is a screen that has been broken into two separate panes that sit side by side. Spatially, the left pane is always thinner than the right pane. Apple leaves the width of the right pane up to the designer but recommends a minimum width of 320 points. Visually, having a larger right pane and a smaller left pane is more balanced. Think about the relationship between the two panes and what information you would like to present in each pane. There usually is a relationship between the two, and it requires some thought and planning to decide how you want users to contextually relate to the information and how you will need to present it.

The left pane is usually referred to as the master pane and the right as the detail pane. This should offer some ideas about how to present your UI elements and information. However, this relationship isn't strictly enforced and refers mostly to orientation and what users may have come to expect as a convention rather than one that is enforced by Apple. A splitview screen can be accessed in either portrait or landscape in iOS7. Figure 4-6 shows a portrait split panel view.

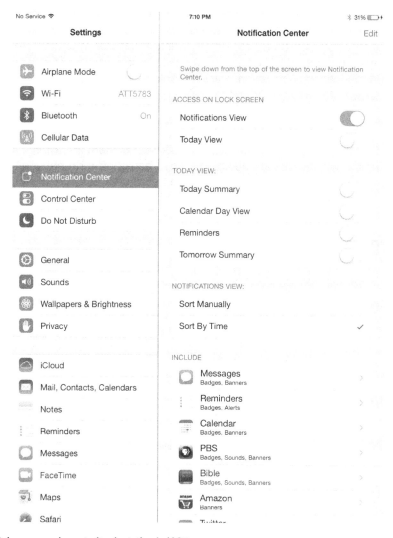

Figure 4-6. The splitview screen in portrait orientation in iOS7

Visual Context

Because of the additional real estate on an iPad, it might be tempting to simply stretch and lengthen your iPhone designs to create your iPad application. Doing so would be a mistake. The added real estate on the iPad means that designers do have more space to, well, . . . design. Menus should be contextual. That is to say, they should be in close proximity to the content to which they are relating. Making users go to the right to edit content on the left will be disorienting. Tools such as popovers should be used when needed and when they help users with the specific task at hand.

Try not to stack too many items at the bottom of the screen or in your tab bar. The sheer size of the iPad makes the bottom of the screen a forgotten area depending on how a user is holding the device. Use the additional elements like popover and split screens to provide context to content.

User Interaction

The iPad's size affords it one particular advantage over the iPhone: users can actually interact with the content using BOTH hands. The keyboard is almost the size of a normal-size computer keyboard, and for those who still think it's too small or uncomfortable, manufacturers have rushed to market with a dizzying number of peripherals that easily connect to the iPad. This means that the opportunities and mechanisms by which users are able to interact with the content in your application has increased. Use this opportunity to draw users into your application for a more immersive experience.

When designing your app, think about orientation and how users will be interacting with your app and the content on the screen. For example, will your app present information better if held in landscape mode only? Or should users be able to move back and forth between portrait and landscape without getting disoriented. It is possible to create a portrait- or landscape-only application.

Onscreen Targets

Since the iPad is used by a variety of users of different ages and sizes, it's a good idea to keep your targets big enough to account for even the largest fingers and thumbs. There's nothing worse than trying to tap a tiny target on a big screen. Also, make sure that targets are obvious. Because of its size, the iPad encourages users to really embrace all facets of multi-touch, and they are more prone to explore the interface. So, making targets obvious and big enough helps users to navigate through your app.

Screen Resolution

Now that the first generation iPad has been discontinued and is no longer supported, there are some significant differences in resolution that are important to keep in mind when designing for the iPads. The remaining iPads available to consumers are the iPad 2 and the iPad Retina. The iPad 2 and iPad Retina share the same screen size (9.5in. x7.31in.) but different resolutions. The iPad 2 has a resolution of 1024 x 768 at 132 pixels per inch (ppi), and the iPad Retina has a resolution of 2048 x 1536 pixels per inch (ppi). This is double the resolution of the iPad 2.

Resolution for iPad Retina display is 2048x1496px (Landscape orientation)

Non-Retina display is 1024x748px (Landscape orientation)

If you're planning to design for the iOS (iPad or iPhone), 72 DPI will worksince DPI is more of a print term anyway.Bear in mind that it is always best to design for Retina and then scale down to 50% of that for non-Retina devices.

The chart in Figure 4-7 lists all of the various resolutions for all devices and has been optimized for iOS 7.

Retina iPad *iPad 3, iPad 4*	1536x2048 px	2048x1536 px
iPad Mini	768x1024 px	1024x768 px
iPad *1st and 2nd Generation*	768x1024 px	1024x768 px

Figure 4-7. Chart shows a list of resolutions for iPad devices

The iPad mini has a smaller screen at 7.87in. x 5.3in. and has a 1024x768 ppi resolution. However, designers shouldn't think that designing for an iPad mini is exactly the same as designing for regular sized iPads. The iPad minis are not only smaller in size, but lighter as well. This will mean that users will interact with the device in a much different way than they do with larger iPads. It's possible, that because of its size, those users will be tempted to use the device with one hand. Think about what this means for the UI of your application. Here are some questions to ask yourself:

How will the size of the device affect the overall experience of my app?

Does the UI of my app need to be different for each device? Or will one layout suffice?

Devices in the same class as the iPad mini include a number of readers like the Nook and Kindle that are used primarily as reading devices as opposed to productivity. Knowing that your app will be available to users of the iPad mini, how does this change the behavior of your application?

Universal Apps

A universal app is an app that is optimized for both the iPad and the iPod. It is like having two apps in one. The assets for both platforms are included in the same app package. Programmatically, the app will determine what platform has been activated and will serve up the appropriate assets for each. Apple recommends that developers create universal apps as it makes it easier to manage for the app store. But, from a design standpoint, there will still be two sets of designs and assets and in essence, this is like creating two separate apps.

Icons

The premise that everything is larger on the iPad also holds true for icons as well. There are a number of different icons for iOS, and all are used differently so that users can recognize your app in the app store and on each different device. Icons for Retina displays will show more detail so make sure that you are resizing for Retina properly.

App Icons

The app icon is what users will see to identify your app both on their device and in the app store. Not only will users visually identify your app by its icon, they will interact with it because they must tap it to launch your application. The app icon is an important branding element. If you are creating a universal app, you will need to create multiple versions of the app icon to include in your app bundle. The sizes are as follows for the iPad:

> 72 x 72 px

> 144 x 144 (hi res)

Remember, all app icons must have 90 degree corners with no rounding, no drop shadows or effects, no shine or gloss. and no alpha transparency. This is even truer with the upcoming release of iOS7. I'll discuss icons in greater detail in Chapter 8. The chart in Figure 4-8 shows all recommended iOS icon sizes from Apple's Human Interface Guidelines.

Description	Size for iPhone 5 and iPod touch (5th generation)	Size for high-resolution iPhone and iPod touch	Size for iPhone and iPod touch	Size for high-resolution iPad	Size for iPad	Guidelines
App icon (required for all apps)	114 x 114	114 x 114	57 x 57	144 x 144	72 x 72	"App Icons"
App icon for the App Store (required for all apps)	1024 x 1024	1024 x 1024	512 x 512	1024 x 1024	512 x 512	"App Icons"
Launch image (required for all apps)	640 x 1136	640 x 960	320 x 480	1536 x 2008 (portrait) 2048 x 1496 (landscape)	768 x 1004 (portrait) 1024 x 748 (landscape)	"Launch Images"
Small icon for Spotlight search results and Settings (recommended)	58 x 58	58 x 58	29 x 29	100 x 100 (Spotlight search results) 58 x 58 (Settings)	50 x 50 (Spotlight search results) 29 x 29 (Settings)	"Small Icons"
Web clip icon (recommended for web apps and websites)	114 x 114	114 x 114	57 x 57	144 x 144	72 x 72	"Web Clip Icons"
Toolbar and navigation bar icon (optional)	Approximately 40 x 40	Approximately 40 x 40	Approximately 20 x 20	Approximately 40 x 40	Approximately 20 x 20	"Icons for Navigation Bars, Toolbars, and Tab Bars"
Tab bar icon (optional)	About 60 x 60 (96 x 64 maximum)	About 60 x 60 (96 x 64 maximum)	About 30 x 30 (48 x 32 maximum)	About 60 x 60 (96 x 64 maximum)	About 30 x 30 (48 x 32 maximum)	"Icons for Navigation Bars, Toolbars, and Tab Bars"
Default Newsstand cover icon for the App Store (required for Newsstand apps)	At least 1024 pixels on the longest edge	At least 1024 pixels on the longest edge	At least 512 pixels on the longest edge	At least 1024 pixels on the longest edge	At least 512 pixels on the longest edge	"Newsstand Icons"

Figure 4-8. Chart shows recommended sizes for all ios icons

Launch Image

The launch image for the iPad should not include the status bar for each region but should provide one for each orientation. Thus:

> Portrait:

> 768 x 1004 px (Non-retina)

> 1536 x 2008 px (Retina)

> Landscape:

> 1024 x 748 px (Non-retina)

> 2048 x 1496 px (Retina)

Remember to add @2x to your file names for hi-res PNGs. We will discuss file naming conventions in more detail in Chapter 9.

iPad-Specific Gestures

Partly because of its size, the iPad has its own set of specific multi-touch gestures.Taking some time to understand these device-specific gestures will go a long way to understanding just how users interact differently with the iPad than they do with the iPhone and how the additional screen space of the iPad lets users do more in terms of interaction and a truly multi-touch and multi-finger experience. These gestures also highlight the fact that the iPad is a true productivity tool and users will expect to do more with. Therefore these gestures are mainly centered around enabling users to navigate and switch between multiple apps at the same time.

In order to use these gestures, users must enable the "multi-tasking gestures" mode from within the Settings ➤ General menu. The gestures enabled here are unique in that they require multiple fingers to activate.

If it so happens that you're still running iOS6 on your iPad, the gestures mentioned below will work but some will yield different results. For instance, the four- or five-fingered swipe upward will reveal the multitasking bar showing apps that are currently open. However, the multitasking bar in iOS6 is different from that in iOS7.

Swipe

A four-finger swipe from left or right will allow the user to cycle through the different apps that are currently open on the iPad. In order for this action to work, you must have at least two apps currently open.

Four-fingered vertical swipe

From any home screen on the iPad, swiping up quickly with four fingers will reveal the multitasking bar that shows all apps that are currently open. You can see the result of the four-finger swipe in iOS7 in Figure 4-9.

Figure 4-9. *The multitasking bar for the iPad as revealed by four-finger swipe in iOS7*

Pinch

Using four fingers to pinch the screen will immediately take the user back to the home screen.

Summary

While the interface of iOS devices is similar, there are different requirements for iPads and iPhones. If you're designing a Universal app that will run on across all iOS devices, you will need to consider each new device, too. When designing your app, orientation, interaction and visual context will all have to be considered to ensure that your users get the best experience possible.Since gestures are the way that users interact with iOS, getting to know what gestures can be used is critical. Your design will need to make the most of the gestures that have become familiar to iOS users; and if you introduce new gestures, make sure that they are explained as users will need to associate them with news tasks in your app.

Chapter 5

Mobile Design Patterns

As developers, most of you are already familiar with the term "design patterns." For developers, design patterns refer to specific software or programming problems that can be solved by using a specific abstract solution. For the purposes of this book, however, we will speak of design patterns as it relates specifically to the design and user interface of your application. Design patterns are helpful ways of addressing common design problems. They are helpful and commonly accepted UI solutions to challenges encountered in mobile design. As mobile evolves, more patterns have emerged to assist designers in addressing common design challenges. As you design your application, you will undoubtedly come upon some of these challenges. Understanding how other designers have found unique and sometimes innovative solutions to these challenges will help you with designing your app by allowing you to focus on functionality as opposed to reinventing the wheel. Because mobile design patterns are accepted best practice solutions that users are familiar with, you adapt them for your application without worrying too much about users being familiar with them.

In this chapter, we'll go through some of the most popular mobile design patterns and break down elements you can use (or not) when implementing them. As with all design elements, users must be the focal point. If a pattern doesn't make your user's life easier, then it's a good idea not to use it. But bear in mind, you can also edit and change patterns to suit your needs. So, it's possible to use an accepted design pattern and still innovate within your application. Using design patterns puts the basic tools into your hands and allows you to establish a starting point in your approach to your design challenge. By viewing how other popular applications have addressed this pattern, it will help you to have a better understanding of how you, too, can address it within your apps. Since design patterns are commonly used across the mobile ecosystem, they are mostly considered to be platform agnostic. So while we are focusing on iOS design for the purpose of this book, you will see patterns being used in native apps and web apps. This is generally considered a good thing as the more widely used a pattern becomes, the greater the chance that users across the board are familiar with it. And from a usability standpoint, this is a good thing.

Many design patterns are available to you, but in this chapter we'll explore just those patterns that are popular and could be helpful.

> **Tip**   If you are more interested in design patterns, it's a good idea to purchase a book written specifically on design patterns. In it, you'll likely find a more exhaustive list than the one included here.

Registration & Login/Sign-up Forms

Registration and sign-up forms are usually the first encounter a user will have with your application. Your overall intent here should be to get the user into your app with minimal fuss. Keep your logins and sign-up pages clean, and use elements of color that align with the overall branding and look and feel of your application. Even though this page will mainly be a field, you can still give your forms personality. One thing to remember is to provide your user with options to login to your app. Some apps have earned significant backlash by making Facebook, Twitter, or some other social media application the only way to gain access to their apps. Bear in mind that some users will not want to connect their social media networks to your app, so provide another option such as e-mail; or better yet, take the opportunity to explain to a user why you are making a social media connection the only option.

Keep the user's privacy in mind and only ask for information that you absolutely need. For example, if your app is a texting or SMS messaging app, you like would need to ask for a user's telephone number. If your app has no need for this information, skip it. It's also a good idea to add popovers to explain why each required item is needed and how it will be used.

Your sign-up or login form pages should also feature a compelling call to action button. Surely, "Register" or "Sign-up" are standard labels, but this can provide an interesting opportunity to show your customers some creativity. Vertical labels placed slightly above the corresponding form fields have also been popular but more recently, especially as apps are updated for iOS7, have been replaced by text directly inside the field. This is easier for users and removes the need for instructional copy elsewhere on the screen.

Unless absolutely necessary, keep your login or sign-up process limited to one screen as the simple wireframe in Figure 5-1 does. Mobile users are notoriously impatient, and everyone is increasingly conscious of their privacy. So a multipage registration will be prohibitive; keep it short and as simple as possible for users to register for your app.

Figure 5-1. *A simple login or sign-in in design pattern*

App Navigation

After a user has signed up or registered for your application, he or she will need to navigate throughout the app. It will be his or her primary means of moving through the app. If you've done a good job, the navigation of your app shouldn't leave users guessing what to do next; their navigation of your app should be intuitive and come naturally. While with the registration and sign-in, patterns are fairly straightforward, navigation offers more options depending on the core functionality and purpose of your apps. If you've explored other apps for inspiration, you will find that there are practically countless ways for navigating through mobile apps. Some patterns lend themselves to specific apps and others have evolved over time along with iOS. Some of the more popular patterns like Sign-up, Springboard, and Image Galleries are listed below, but there are new patterns like the Slide-out Navigation that are being created all the time. iOS is still relatively new and as designers begin to push the boundaries of design, expect new patterns to emerge. So, if your app is a social media app that will have users moving through a specific hierarchy or a feed of friends and information, you may want to stick to the established design patterns in use by popular apps. Users will already by familiar with these patterns and will expect you to follow suit.

Springboard or Home Screen Patterns

One of the most popular design patterns for navigating within an app is the springboard pattern. The springboard is a grid of icons on the home page that visually acclimates users to all of the content in your application. It provides a high-level overview of all of the content in your app for the user from one page. The springboard will be the first page a user sees after he or she loads your app and registers or signs in. It familiarizes users with all of the content in the app and provides context for them. You can consider or use the springboard page as a home page that users will come back to time and time again in order to access other areas of your application. Thus, the information you choose to include on the springboard is critical. It is important to note that the amount of icons you can include on the springboard is limited to about nine (depending on layout), so make sure that if you feature multiple pages, your users know how to access them.

Even though we are speaking of iOS specifically, it's important to note that the springboard is considered to be a cross platform approach to navigation as the springboard can easily be adapted for many different types of devices and operating systems. Figure 5-2 shows an example of a simple springboard mock-up.

Figure 5-2. A simple wireframe of a springboard design pattern

There have been multiple variations on the springboard design pattern – meaning that even though the mock-up above shows a grid layout, you are free to customize the layout in a way that is consistent with the look and feel of your app.

Take the opportunity to get creative with the icons in your springboard. Icons will provide context for your users, as each icon will visually represent a separate functionality within the app. The springboard is an easy way to provide a considerable amount of information for users all on one page, and It will be the first time that users will be exposed to the visual language of your app.

Sometimes a springboard may not follow the popular grid layout, and icons may be larger or smaller than the standard nine-icon layout. Decide what's best for your user and works best with your app's style to identify the best springboard layout for you. It must be noted as well that the springboard pattern can be viewed as somewhat dated as newer, more innovative home screen patterns have emerged to show various options from a home screen.

Many news apps such as CNN and TED feature the front page pattern. It features a large panel on top with a list view underneath and is a popular way to display news from the home page of an app.

List & Table View Patterns

Another popular approach to mobile navigation is to put everything in a list menu. A list menu is a great option for apps that have lots of categories and content. It will appear in a table view.Part of what makes the list menu so perfect for mobile apps is that a scrollable list is easy to flick up and down with the thumb or two fingers. So, in terms of navigation and usability, the list menu is a winner. List menus can feature icons like the springboard menu so that users can visually relate to the content in your app as well.

Within the interface of an iOS mobile device, there are a number of variations on the list menu pattern.

You can enhance and customize lists by changing their colors or by adding images and icons. But be careful not to overdo it and disorient users.

Tables

Tables are a great way to display information in apps that will feature lots of data. Many enterprise, productivity, banking, and finance tools will likely need to use lots of tables as they will need to list information in a way that is legible and easily sorted. There a quite a few different tables that you can use when designing your app. If you are showing a significant amount of data and need a way to differentiate between them, try changing the colors or adding subtle variances between them. This will help your users as they sift through the information being presented.

When designing for iOS, consider a table another name for the table view. This element is outlined clearly in the Human Interface Guidelines.

You can make adjustments to your tables to make the data more palatable for your users. Rows and columns can be adjusted for size, and you can consider experimenting with the size of the font to segment specific information for your users. For instance, consider experimenting with headers and with grouping rows for easier navigability.

You might also consider visual enhancements such as icons to make data in a table pop. It's a good idea not to feature too many different colors in a single table, so as with everything, keep your table color scheme consistent with your overall branding. However, if your app falls into a specific category, use well-established best practices such as green for positive cash flow and red for negative in finance or money management apps. Users will be well acquainted with these visuals, and this will lend to the overall usability of your app.

For tables with a significant amount of information, the fixed columns design pattern can be helpful. This pattern allows users to freeze a single column on the left or right while the other columns remain fluid. Users can then adjust at will and sort through information as needed.

Tabs

You can also add the tab bar navigation to your iOS app if you choose. On iOS devices, the tab bar is located on the bottom of the screen and device, but some creative designers have managed to put tab bars at the top of the screen as well. You are able to customize the tab bar in iOS apps but refer to the Human Interface Guidelines for specifics. For instance, only five buttons are allowed in the tab bar of the iPhone iPod. More are possible; they just won't be shown. iOS will automatically add a "More" button where users will be able to access the others. From a usability standpoint, tab bars are easy to access by users using their thumbs while holding smaller devices such as phones.

Each button in a tab bar can reference a completely different view that relates to various types of information in your app. The convenience factor of the tab bar navigation makes it easy for users to be able to switch back and forth between them all quite easily and with very little effort. By adding a tab bar, a user will be able to have a high-level view of all of the various categories of your application from one page.

Each button in the tab bar usually features an icon and a label like the wireframe in Figure 5-3 shows. Icons are a great way to convey information; but because the icons in the tab bar will be close in proximity, it is a good idea to make sure that they are visually consistent for your users. If one button is drawn or illustrated in a particular style, then make sure that all of the others follow suit as well. Your users will expect it.

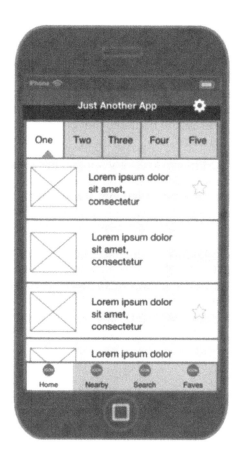

Figure 5-3. Tab bars in iOS

Tab bar buttons must have different states as this will help users to understand when they are have activated a button and within that section's view. Even with the new "floating" tab bar in iOS 7, you will need to, as with all buttons, provide feedback and visual cues to your users so that they know when a button in the bar has been activated. For the tab bar, this can be achieved programmatically.

Slide-Out Navigation

Recently, a new kind of mobile design pattern has emerged called the slide-out navigation. Popular apps like Facebook, Gmail for iOS, and Path have made this design pattern a new standard. But Facebook, in the redesigned version of its original iOS app, introduced the new pattern and it has been quickly adopted by others. It consists of a panel that is revealed by sliding the main content area to the right. That main panel area, then, reveals a new list view underneath that users can navigate through for additional content and views.

The slide-out navigation can be revealed or activated by tapping a list button in the upper left hand corner of the app and then closed by tapping the same button or by the user swiping back to the left or right. In some apps, like Gmail for iPhone, the panel is initiated with a back button. This could be confusing for users, so it might be best to stick with the widely used list or menu button. This is a button that features three or four horizontal lines and somewhat resembles a table view. Note that when the menu button is activated, the panel as well as the button must all slide to the right and remain partially visible, allowing the user to quickly undo the action should he or she need to. Tapping an item in the new menu, however, will reveal the content related to that menu, item and the panel will disappear completely to reveal the contents that correspond to that menu item. Tapping the menu button will bring the panel back.

The slide-out navigation solution isn't useful for every app, so think about its use. If your app is content heavy, then this type of navigation is for you. Even so, it is considered a secondary navigation solution. Thus, the more important elements should be at the top level view in the app's hierarchy where users can access them easily. But it is a great tool for allowing users to jump around as they please.

Some new apps like Jawbone's UP app has taken this trend even further by having a slide-out navigation on both the left and right sides of the screen. Apps that use this feature are usually content heavy and so the dual slide navigation is a great way to segment content and functionality of your app. If you use the double slide-out navigation, make sure that your content is grouped contextually so that users know what they will find on each panel.

Image Gallery

The image gallery navigation is great for segmenting content and presenting it in a visual way, usually with photographs as representatives for news stories and other content that changes often or tends to be frequently updated. The image gallery pattern lets users browse visually and uses images instead of icons. Image galleries can be easily navigated by scrolling through the images. For apps with lots of content, an image gallery is an easy, convenient, and engaging way to browse. Popular image apps like Instagram and 500px use this pattern to allow users to quickly navigate visual content.

Searching and Sorting

If your app offers a search or sort feature, depending on the kind of app it is, it could very well be one of the most important aspects of your app. iOS offers the ability to search in a number of its stock applications. The Phone and Messages apps are shown in Figure 5-4. It's a good idea to replicate theses search patterns in your app as users will already be familiar with the way that they work. Even if it seems obvious to you, make sure that search fields are labeled, either with the word search or with the familiar search icon (usually a magnifying glass). If a user will need to find the search function, he or she will not want to look far and wide for it. Making it easily recognizable will help.

Figure 5-4. *The Phone app's search feature*

iOS 7 now offers users the ability to search their devices directly from the springboard. Once initiated, the user can begin to type a query and the results of the search are populated below. This Spotlight search features a cancel button to the right of the search field whether or not the user has typed a query. However, in the Mail app, the search bar is persistent from within any mailbox. The cancel button will only appear once the user begins to type the query. Either of these patterns is acceptable. But naturally, if your application is an e-mail app, I would follow the Mail pattern closely to avoid having users relearn how to perform this task specifically for your app.

Some other search-related patterns are, in my opinion, fairly obvious but I will state them here anyway. Listing your results dynamically even as a user is typing is a nice touch as is segmenting them where necessary so that users can easily scan through for what they need. This is handled nicely in the iOS 7 Spotlight search. Search results are listed directly below the search box and show users the location of the results on the device and in alphabetical order. Thus, a "seri" search will yield results in Events, Mail, Messages, and anywhere else there is a matching term as is shown in Figure 5-5.

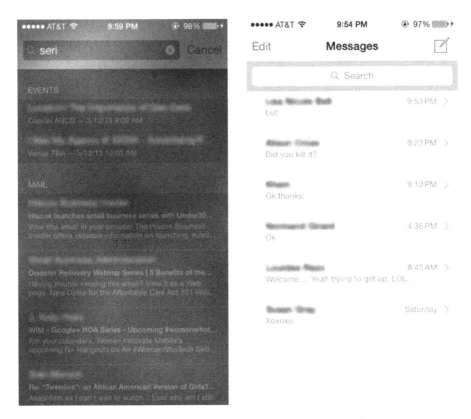

Figure 5-5. The search functionality in the spotlight search and in the Mail app works slightly differently

Sorting is usually performed after the search query has been completed and results have been displayed. Depending on the results, there are a few eloquent ways used to allow users to sort search results. For large result data sets, users may be required to sort results even more than the initial query. Segmenting results into chunks will allow users to further filter the results of their initial query. If you choose this route, it is important to name sections carefully to avoid confusing your users. For instance, you might be working on a location-based app that shows the user the nearest restaurant serving burgers. If you are displaying location-based results for such a business query for your users and your location is densely populated with burger joints yielding lots of businesses, you might want to further segment the results to allow users to sort nearby results (within a certain radius) as opposed to a huge list all of the results. So, an acceptable way to further segment these results would be within radii of 5 miles. Users will then be able to view businesses within 5 miles, 10 miles, 15 miles, and so on.

Tips, Tours, and Walkthroughs

If your app features a unique user interface or functionality that might not be entirely intuitive for users, you can add tips or a tour to walk users through the less intuitive parts of the application. A tour will guide users step-by-step through specific actions while a tip will add context to specific features that a user might not familiar with. In both instances, both of these patterns usually take place when a user is interacting with your app for the first time. Some apps, however, make the tip or walkthrough available to the users from within the app should they need to familiarize themselves with features that may be difficult to learn.

Tips and tours fall under the Help design pattern. While there are others in this category, we will focus on these two for the purposes of this book.

Tips can be used liberally throughout an app and pretty much on any screen. If your app has a feature that you would like to call attention to, a tip is a non-obtrusive way to do so. By this time, users are accustomed to tips and how they work. Tips can be initiated by a button or other hotspot on the user's screen. If a tip is contained in a popover, then tapping anywhere on the screen outside of the tip popover should make it disappear. If you're using the standard popover element, you will want to place the tip near the feature you are referencing. Finally, keep the copy in your tip concise. A tip filled with detailed instructions can be overwhelming to your users so keep the instruction short and to the point. Figure 5-6 shows how to create a tip with enough information so as not to overwhelm your user.

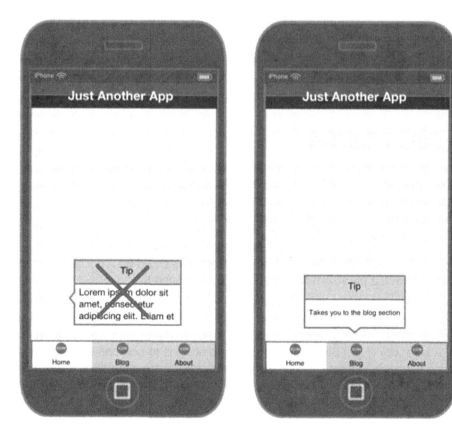

Figure 5-6. If using a popover for a tip, make sure that the tip follows the rules of using a popover and that it contains just the right amount of information

A tour or walkthrough is more detailed than a tip and provides the user with more information in the form of a guided step-by-step instruction through the application. It will automatically appear at the beginning of an app and take users through a detailed process in the app. With a tour, while users are moving through the app at their own speed, you are responsible for the path they will take. You will have lots of opportunities to be creative in the tour and to make it engaging for your users. With a tour, it is important to keep the information as the focal point. It is not necessary to point out functionality that users should be familiar with. Keep your tour focused on the unique aspects of the app. If your app features many levels of interaction and can engage different kinds of users, then the tour is a great way to showcase specific tasks that will enhance their experience.

Like the tip, the tour should be an experience that is easily exited should the user decide to leave or another activity such as a phone call interrupts the process. A user should also be aware of how much longer the tour will last either by a visual cue such as a page indicator.

Another good rule of thumb is to keep your tours as visual as possible with copy and text being used in a balanced, yet minimal way. That is to say that the amount of copy should never overwhelm the visuals on the screen. Use your visuals as a part of the story as opposed to patronizing users by pointing out every aspect of your app with an explanation. If you are overly dependent on words to explain a feature, then that feature must be reexamined. Consider the tour to be the perfect combination of words and visuals to explain how to interact with your app.

Your creativity can take center stage with tips and tours, too. Design effects such as opacity and translucency (a favorite of iOS 7) can enhance the look and feel of your tours and bring them to life in a richer, more interactive way.

Stepping Out of the Box

If you choose to be original and create an entirely new approach to an already established pattern, be careful. A new approach to an old problem where design patterns already exist could be a risky maneuver. If you decide to step out of the design pattern box, test your new approach against the old one and allow your users to provide feedback. Since testing can get complicated and can also be time consuming, a simple way to test your new approach would be to take a small subset of your users and allow them to interact with your new pattern as well as the old one and gather their feedback. If your test group prefers the old design pattern, this could be a good indicator that it's probably best to stick with a paradigm that users are accustomed to.

Always use standard iOS elements. The Human Interface Guidelines provide iOS-specific elements that easily replace standard web elements. One of the biggest mistakes that designers make is to introduce web elements into their mobile designs. These elements can work against you and frustrate users. A sure way to get bad reviews in the app store is to confuse users by mixing metaphors—using elements in your UI incorrectly. Breadcrumbs are a common web paradigm used to show users where they are in content-heavy sites. However, the back button in iOS replaces a long list of previous pages that can be displayed on a website.

Summary

Design patterns are accepted solutions to common design problems. You can use them liberally in your application to help to speed up the design process considerably. Patterns exist for the registration and sign-in process, primary and secondary navigation, search, sorting and help. There are many other design patterns that exist. The Human Interface Guidelines is a great place to start to become even more familiar with design patterns and how to implement them specifically for your iOS application. You can also improvise with patterns, but be sure to test them rigorously with users. Improvising doesn't mean reinventing the wheel.

Using Wireframes to Design Your App

Whether you're designing for the web or for a mobile device, it is always good to prepare a wireframe to help you flesh out all of the functionality of your app.

A great way to think of a wireframe is like an architectural blueprint for a building. It's a common example. As we all know, blueprints must be completed before the building can actually be built. In the same way, wireframes should be created before you move into the actual design or development phase of creating the app, and is fundamental to the process.

Everything we've done so far in this book has led you to this point. Where you're actually creating something. You've done your due diligence; you've crafted your idea from *just* an idea to an actual product. You've talked to potential users and validated your idea against others in the app store. You've compared your app to its competition in the category and you've solicited feedback to understand where you stand; and now, you're ready to create your app. How exciting!

Now, we'll actually start to take the necessary steps toward creating your application. That starts with wireframing. We will start with sketches and discuss various tools that can help with the prototyping and user interaction of your application. We will continue to use our Travel Light app as a test case and develop wireframes for the application as well.

What Is a Wireframe?

A wireframe is a simple drawing of your application (web or mobile) that outlines all of the interface elements and functionality before you get to the proper design phase of the application. It is usually devoid of branding or color. The wireframe is a great way to become intimately familiar with everything that your app does when users interact with it (see Figure 6-1).

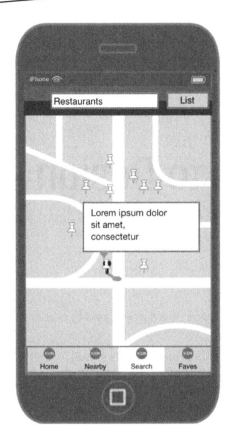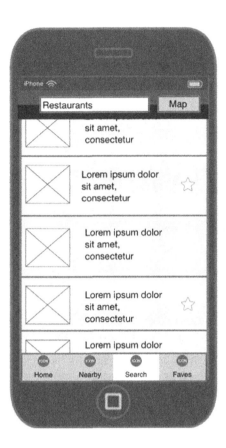

Figure 6-1. A wireframe is a drawing of your app with all of its interface elements

Wireframes are all about usability and interactivity. After your wireframing process is complete, you should know the result of every action a user performs while using your app.

At the completion of the wireframing phase of the app development process, you should know and be able to answer the following questions about your app:

> What happens when a user taps on any button in the app?
>
> What is the best and most intuitive route for each task in the app?
>
> Does the app use established best practices in its user interface?
>
> Are tasks completed using the smallest amount of steps possible?
>
> Does the user understand the tasks he or she is performing and why?
>
> Have all possible use cases been explored and accounted for?

Wireframes will often be devoid of color and branding. This can make them easier to read. Adding branding and color can sometimes distract from the purpose of the wireframe, and that is to outline and finalize functionality before the design and polish has been added to the application. Wireframes are also great because they allow for easy iterating in case changes need to be made to the interface of the design of your app. If your wireframing is moving along optimally, you will find that you will have a number of versions of your wireframes before the entire process has been completed. This is a good thing as as each version of your wireframes should improve on the previous version.

Some wireframes are more polished than others and how polished yours are can depend on a number of factors. If you are creating your app for a client, then they might want to see a certain level of polish or professionalism to the wireframes. If this is not an absolute requirement, then I would suggest that you keep your wires black and white, and use the simplest presentation possible.

Tools for Wireframing

There are a number of online resources and tools for creating wireframes. There are also mobile-specific wireframing tools. A search can for "wireframing tools" will yield articles featuring lists of available tools for wireframing. Some of them will be web based, app based, downloadable, free, paid, and open source. You will need to find what works best for you. Of the web-based variety, here is a list of my top three:

1. JustinMind – Lets users create clickable, interactive mobile wireframes that allow sharing for feedback.

2. Proto.io – Allows users to create wireframes that can be used for protyping and testing. Supports sharing and on-device viewing. Free - $49 per month.

3. MoqUps – A free HTML 5-based wireframing tool that allows iOS templates to allow users to create simple fast mobile app wires.

If you don't mind paying a little more, here's another list of wireframing tools that will set you back some cash:

1. Omnigraffle - $99.99 for an individual license. Available for Mac and on iPad – A Mac user favorite, Omnigraffle lets you create not only apps and websites, but also many different types of diagrams and charts.

2. iMockups - $6.99 in the iPad App store – iPad app that allows creation of wireframes for apps and sites from within an intuitive iPad interface. The app could use an update but is a great tool for creating basic app wireframes.

3. Balsamiq – Downloadable wireframing tool that provides sketch-based wireframes from an easy-to-use interface. Also supports sharing for feedback. $79 for a single license.

Again, these lists are based on my personal preferences. Most of these products provide users with the option to try them out before making a commitment, so I encourage you to try them all if you can. Make sure that whichever app you choose allows you to export your wireframes in a few different formats. You'll need at least one of the popular image formats (JPEG, PNG) and the ever-popular PDF. Another feature that might be helpful is the abilty to collaborate and share your wires with others. This will help when you are soliciting feedback from colleagues, team members, and potential users.

You may also choose to skip web-based and other digital tools altogether and simply choose to do it the old fashioned way. That is, pen or pencil and a piece of paper. There are stencils you can find online that will provide the iPhone or iPad frame so that you can fill in the necessary UI elements for your app. Either way, wireframing and ideation is an important step in the app design process and not one to be skipped.

Why Are Wireframes Important?

Naturally, at this point, you might be eager to get to the act of designing your application. You're thinking of color and shading and translucency and what kind of details you would like to include in your app icon. But not so fast. While not entirely appealing from a design standpoint, getting through the wireframing process is important, as it will help to inform the actual design. Once your wireframes are complete, you will find that your design and development will flow smoother than if you hadn't completed this step in the process.

Wireframes are important because they help with creating the layout and help you to organize the information in your app for the user. During this process, you are free to do and to undo; try different approaches to solving a particular usability problem in your app. If something doesn't work, you can easily discard it and not worry about branding and other details just yet. This is especially liberating because with the pixel perfect precision needed for design, you won't want to deal with usability issues. You will need the flexibility that wireframing provides if you decide to scrap a screen or flow altogether. If you're not committed to colors and design, then you can focus on layout, usability, and flow, which should be your main focus when wireframing.

If you are working with a client, you will also find that wireframes are a great way to get sign-off on the user interface and other elements before you progress to style and design. That way, your client knows exactly what to expect and your design can add depth to the wires.

The Wireframing Process

The first step in wireframing your application is to begin to think about the layout of your app. There has been some discussion about the best way to do this. If you have downloaded one of the templates mentioned earlier you can use one of those. Personally, I'm partial to paper. While it sounds decidedly low tech, paper is easy to use and easy to correct mistakes should you make them. The other great thing about paper is that it's tangible. You can touch and feel paper and for some designers, mapping things out on paper before moving to a digital medium helps the ideation process. Whiteboards are also good for ideating your apps. You can use dry erase markers to easily map out ideas and correct mistakes. You might also be interested in using preprinted stencils that you can sketch interface items into. I find paper and stencils can be extremtly liberating. Copying the stencils or outlines and making multiple copies is one way to do it. Or, as with everything else, you can find downloadable stencils online free of charge. If not, then use the wireframing tool of your choice. I've included a device outline in Figure 6-2. This along with the ones in Figure 6-3 might be helpful if you decide to go the paper route. I tend to make a few copies with one frame on each page with space on either side for my notes. If I'm not inclined to make copies or use a stencil, I'll draw everything freehand and make the stencils the second step in my wireframing process. That way, the freehand designs will count as the first draft of the wireframes until some of the basic layout and usability issues have been resolved.

Figure 6-2. *A simple iPhone outline*

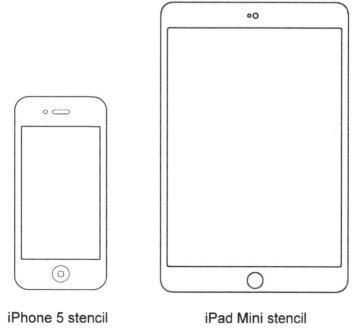

iPhone 5 stencil   iPad Mini stencil

Figure 6-3. *Basic stencils for the iPhone 5 and the iPad mini. These can be used for wireframing apps*

To begin your wireframing process, you should have everything that you have collected up until this point: the description of your app that should now be refined to include the feedback you received from your validation as well as the apps that show best practices and design patterns that illustrate the common functionality within your application. If there are no design patterns that apply to every screen, that's fine: you will have to create them.

If you choose to go with an electronic or web-based wireframing tool, as with the paper stencil above, you want to at least begin your wireframing process with an outline of the iPhone or iPad depending on which device your app is for. Your wireframing program of choice should include this frame or outline. It doesn't have to be realistic, but the dimensions should be exact so that you are working with the appropriate aspect ratio for the device you are designing for.

Before you put pen to paper or actually begin to map out your user interface, be sure to put yourself into the mindset of a user, not a designer or developer. The overall purpose of the app and needs of the intended user should guide the development of your wireframes. The user must be at the heart of every step of the process. As the designer, you might feel the need to add funky, new elements to your interface and experiment with your layout. However, if it doesn't work for your user and the task they are trying to perform, your app won't be successful. It is really important as a designer and developer to remove yourself from the process and to be able to put yourself in the shoes of your user. This is why your app statement is important. By this time, you should be able to refer to the statement created in Chapter 1 to guide you in the wireframing process.

An Information Architect or (IA) will sometimes create wireframes but it is not uncommon for them to be also done by designers these days.

> **Tip** An Information Architect is a person that creates blueprints and wireframes for a website or application.

In some instances, the lines between IA and Designer have been blurred. If you identify as a designer in its purest form, it is a good idea to become familiar with usability and the best way to do so is to create wirerames for your apps. If you can find an IA or UX person to work with you; that's even better. But if not, you should be able to use some of the the tools in this chapter to create your wireframes.

Focus on Usability

Wireframing is all about usability. Therefore, it is important ask yourself some critical questions during the wireframing process.

- What is the first task that the user will need to perform after opening your app?
- From any given screen, what is the most important task for the user?
- What information does the user need on the current screen to inform his or her task?
- Based on existing patterns and best practices, what will the user expect to see at this juncture?
- If a task contains multiple steps, what is the best and shortest path for this task?

If we continue with our original idea of creating a travel app that helps users pack light for their trips like we did in Chapter 1, we will need to ask ourselves key questions about the user and what he or she will need to inform the tasks for the app. If you're doing a good job of designing your app, you will have followed those steps, too, and should be able to get the answers from those questions there.

For example, does your user need to sign in or register to use the app? If so, grabbing a design pattern might be best. What information do you need to collect here? There is no real need here to reinvent the wheel with sign-in and registration. Users are familiar with this process so remember to collect only the information that you need and sketch out the input fields and confirmation for this process. Is the app pulling information from social networks? If so, then, you know that you will need to ask users' permission to do so. Remember, that your goal is to get the user past this process as quickly as possible so that he or she can begin to interact with your app. Refer back to registration and login mobile design pattern best practices in Chapter 5 if you need to. Keep it simple because you'll want to get users actually using your app. If the registration process is too complicated, you will lose users who may never return. Your goal at this point is to get them into the app in the fewest steps possible.

Try Various Layouts

Experiment with different layouts, too. The first layout that pops into your head will certainly not be the last. But get it down as a starting point. The goal is to get something on paper that begins the process. Try to complete your wireframes in order. This means trying to map out pages and screens in the same order that you expect a user to while using your app. One way to do this is to separate the various sections of the application by each task and subtask associated with the various creens in your app. That way, you have a clear idea of what you're wireframing.

As an example, we've created an app called Travel Light. We'll use the app to illustrate examples of the various techniques and steps in the design process throughout the book.

Outline User Flow

Every app has a flow. This is the way that the user will move through the application. You should at least have a few ideas of how this will work for your app. It will make creating the user flow much easier. Some of the wireframing tools above can also be used to create user flows. However, any tool that allows you to draw basic shapes will work just fine. The easiest and simplest way to start the user flow process is to simply make a list of all of the major tasks you can think of that are associated with your application. Be as specific as possible here. This is where your application begins to come to life. You can write each step on a Post-it note so that you can move them around when you figure out an additional step that may have to be inserted between two others. Or, you can write each step out on a whiteboard, too. The purpose of the user flow is to trace the path that the user must take to complete a specific task. As you are working on your user flow, you should ask and be able to answer the following questions:

- Who is the user and what does he or she need?
- Why is the user interacting with the app?
- Where is the user going?

- What is ultimate objective of this task?

- What is the user's goal?

- What is the purpose of the app?

- Is there a specific business objective? (In app purchases or sales)

- Where does the task begin and where does it end?

Below, I've attempted to answer the above questions for our Travel Light application. Note that each answer is simple. As you work on your wireframes your answers could change, too.

Who is your user and what does he or she need?

The Travel Light user is a busy traveler who needs to know exactly what to take on each trip.

Why is your user interacting with the app?

The user is interacting with Travel Light to minimize his or her carry-on luggage and ensure that he or she only has what is needed.

Where is your user going?

The user is going to create a new list.

What is the ultimate objective of this task?

The ultimate goal of this task is to help the user to create a list and associate it with a particular trip.

What is the user's goal?

The ultimate goal is to create a complete list for the given trip.

What is the purpose of the app?

The purpose of the app is to allow users to take only what they need while not forgetting anything.

Is there a specific business objective? (In app purchases or sales)

Ultimately, we will link users to other partners that offer low-cost travel solutions.

Where does the task begin and where does it end?

The main tasks begin with entering trip details such as a departure and destination city and date. The task ends when a user has selected all of his or her items for a particular trip.

Figure 6-4 shows an example of a very basic user flow for the Travel Light app.

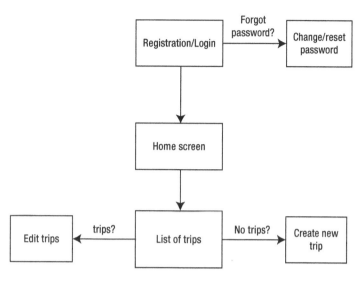

Figure 6-4. *The user flow for the Travel Light app lays out the major tasks and paths that a user could take as he or she navigates the app*

Now that we've created a list of needs of our user, we can begin to put write the major tasks associated with completing those goals we've just outlined.

In order to create the screens from our Travel Light app, our list of major tasks and subtasks might look like this:

> Tap app icon
>
> Registration and Sign-in page
>
>> Choose and enter user name (E-mail address)
>>
>> Choose and enter password
>>
>> Click sign-in button

If we were to outline all of the steps associated with entering details around a trip, the list might look like this:

> Trip entry
>
>> Enter trip details; City, state, airport, date, and time of departure
>>
>>> Ask to use current location; if yes, list associated airports
>>>
>>> If no, user may enter manually
>>>
>>> User chooses departure airport
>>>
>>> User enters date from calendar popup
>>>
>>> User enters time from picker?
>>
>> Save trip details – User should be able to edit trip details

List creation & confirmation

>   User creates new packing list – new list is associated with new trip

>   User adds new items to list

>   User may also select items from older lists or popular items

>   App suggests items over time if user has forgotten, based on previous lists/trips

Ancillary tasks in the Settings panel might be:

Settings

>   Enable location-based services

>   Alerts? (Badges, notification center, sounds, etc.)

The previous list is by no means exhaustive, nor is it complete. There may very well be some steps missing. It is simply a first stab at the tasks associated with creating wireframes for this fictional application. A list such as this is what should inform the first iteration of wireframes.

The screens in Figure 6-5 show some basic sketches of how our Travel Light wireframes might look for the registration and trip entry portion of our fictional application. The tasks below represent tasks that a new user would perfom in the app. It was created freehand and without using any stencils. Even though it is in rough shape, you will be able to make out the elements of the user interface and some of the critical sections for each screen. You can do the same for your app, or use a stencil. Either way, you must try to map your screens and user interface elements to your tasks. As you work through the screens, gaps and missing steps should become apparent. When they do, you will be able to fill them in.

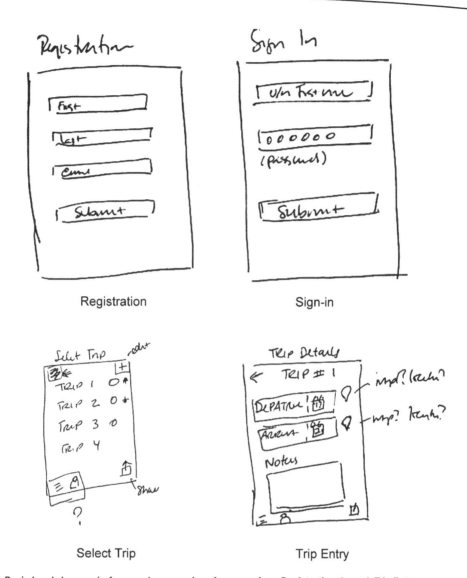

Figure 6-5. *Basic hand-drawn wireframes show a series of screens from Registration through Trip Entry*

Once you've reviewed your sketches, Post-its, or stencils against your task list, various user paths will also begin to emerge. For our Travel Light app, we've covered some of the tasks that every user has to perform such as register and add trips, and create lists. These are considered primary tasks. Along the way, however, there will be some secondary tasks that may arise as well. These are tasks that may or may not be apparent or necessary for all users but will need to be a part of the flow for others. These tasks—major and minor—will start to reveal different use cases for your app.

Define Use Cases

As you move through the wireframing process with your user at the center of the work, you may find that your users are not all the same and do not have the same needs as they interact with your app. Most apps I have seen have at least two use cases. Use cases are also sometimes called user stories. They help you to craft a unique experience for your application based on who you understand that user to be and what their needs are. This will frame how you create the UI of your app.

When wireframing around specific use cases, you will need to define those user interface elements that are most intuitive for that particular user. Say, for instance, that we have a power user for our Travel Light app. This user travels often and has already saved multiple trips in the app. How then, would this user's experience differ from a new user? Based on that use case, this user flow might progress this way:

1. Open app

2. Select from list of previous trips or add new trip if not already listed

3. Import list from another trip

4. Edit list if needed

5. Confirm

Note that this use case is much different from the initial use case that laid out the tasks for a new user in the wireframes above. A power or recurring user will already be familiar with the functionality of the application, its interface, and how to perform critical tasks. So, in the wireframes for this flow (Figure 6-6), we will make basic assumptions about how this user will interact with the app and what he or she will expect to see when performing specific tasks.

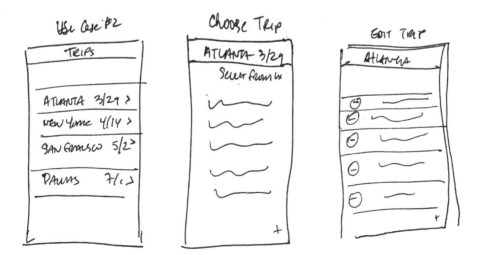

Figure 6-6. Wireframes for a specific use case

Add Wireframe Details

Once you have mapped out your blocks and user interface, you can begin to add more details to your wireframes. Label buttons if you need to and add title headers to screens so that they begin to come to life. Think again, about how users will be able to recognize the UI elements, and associate them with the tasks at hand. Ask questions like the following:

- What elements of iOS's user interface would be best to use?

- When selecting dates, would a date picker be best? Or would it be easier to present a calendar that will allow users to see the month laid out before them for easier selection?

- Is time a consideration for your users? Will they be using your app while multitasking?

- Where are users most likely to be using your app?

- Are users likely to be on the go or in motion while using your app? If so, how will that affect how you arrange critical UI elements like buttons?

- Will your user more like to be using your app with one hand, or two?

The answers to these questions will affect not only the flow, but also the layout of your application. This is where you begin to refine the UI of your app.

As mentioned before, wireframing is an iterative process. You will likely do multiple versions of your wires before they are final. However, each version should bring you closer to your final one and prepare you for the actual design phase.

Share Wireframes for Feedback

If you can, it is always a good idea to share your wireframes with others, too. Much like your initial statement for your app, wireframes are pretty much useless unless they are shared. You can't design in a box. Share your wireframes with either your friends or colleagues, or, if at all possible, with potential users.

If you can, create a small user base and get them to review the early wires and collect their feedback, using it to refine the wires further. If you are able to get the same group who evaluated the app statement to also weigh in and provide feedback on the wireframes, that would be ideal. You will be working with a group that is familiar with the overall concept of the app and its functionality. For this audience, seeing the app evolve over time can be helpful and insightful for you as the designer.

Be careful with user feedback, however. There can be times when user feedback flies in the face of accepted best practices. If this is the case with some of the feedback you receive, weigh this feedback seriously before implementing – especially if it goes counter to accepted best practices or known design patterns. For example, many travel apps present a user with a monthly calendar for selecting dates for travel. If, during focus group, a user or users decided that another way would be better, you might want to weigh the pros and cons of such a decision. The reason being is that your core users may very well expect to see that calendar when they try to enter dates. The picker for iOS is a great way to allow users to select dates and time. But, If your alternative to the calendar isn't user friendly or intuitive, you may want to disregard this specific feedback and stick with what's known and used universally.

For specific animations or implied movement in your app's wireframes, you will need to show users the pre- and post-animation state since wireframes are mostly static. If you're going low fidelity, then pre- and post-animation states *as well as* detailed annotations should be fine to illustrate movement. Some users won't know what certain transitions mean either; so showing them visually is one way to avoid confusing users in your focus group when soliciting feedback.

Create Prototypes

Some of the popular wireframing software on the market will allow you to create a clickable prototype of your app that you can run on an actual device. Of the ones listed earlier, Proto.io, JustinMind, and iMockups will let you create some sort of clickable prototype. They can be a great way to show your users precisely how the app will work. Others may only let you interact with the app in a web interface. Any wireframing tool that replicates real interactivity that users will experience with your app is great for testing, but not absolutely necessary. It is possible to get great feedback from static, paper wireframes as well as interactive wireframes and there is even a tool called POP (Prorotyping on Paper) shown in Figure 6-7 that lets you take pictures of your paper wireframes and add some interactivty to them. It is available as an app and looks fun to use. Ideally, the best approach would be to allow users to interact directly with your app from a device for which it is being designed.

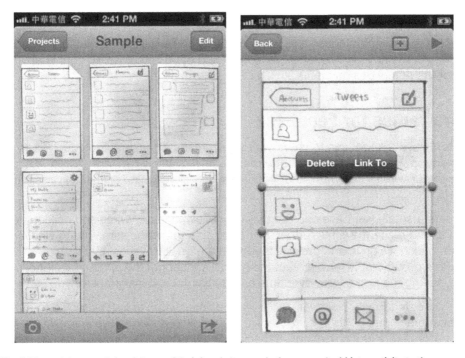

Figure 6-7. The POP app lets users take pictures of their hand-drawn wireframes and add interactivity to them

Clients and Wireframes

If you are creating an app for yourself as a designer-developer, your wireframes will be mostly for your eyes only. Barring your sharing with others for feedback, you can pretty much set the level of polish you apply to your wireframes. If you are dealing with a client, however, your wireframes may benefit from annotations and some level of guidance for your clients. As wireframes are devoid of any branding or color, clients might find them difficult to read. Before presenting wireframes to clients, let them know what to expect. Annotate the wireframes with directions, and if possible, walk your clients through the flow. Sending wireframes to clients that don't understand them is a sure way to delay sign-off and can result in endless feedback loops that create more questions and clarification than actual approval.

You will rarely share hand-drawn wireframes like the ones in Figures 6-4 and 6-5 with a client. But, they are a great start for iterating internally if you have a team. And even though I've reviewed and listed wireframing software and tools, you are under no pressure to use them. The wireframes in Figure 6-8 are a better example of what would be acceptable to send to a client for review.

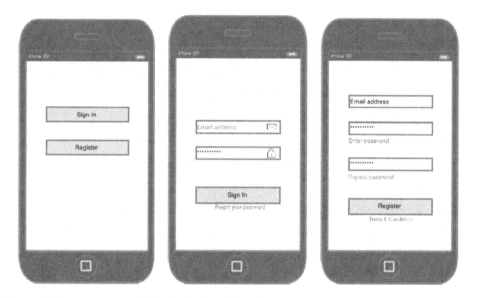

Figure 6-8. These wireframes are more suitable for sharing with a client

In addition to being more polished, they are easier to read and thus understand. Because your wireframes will represent every page of your application and ideally show how users will interact with what they see on each screen, it is a good idea to include every element that the user will see by the time he or she gets to your final wires. Note the "Forgot your password" and "Terms & Conditions" links in the screens above. While not shown here, it is not uncommon to show the user flow that users will experience for retrieving a lost password.Sometimes, Terms & Conditions are shown in a web view in apps as they tend to change and this allows for easy updates. If your T&C's require user action such as tapping the "Agree" button in order to move forward, then show those screens as well.

Summary

Your wireframes are a critical part of the design process. They will help you to create the user flow and to define the overall experience that users will have with your application. The main purpose for wireframes is to allow you to create user-centric scenarios that will provide the best overall experience for users of your application. Make sure that your wireframes are answering key questions about how and why users are interacting with the app. If you're having trouble getting started, you can always refer to design patterns, which we discussed in Chapter 6; or your initial app statement for your app. There are multiple tools available on the market for the purpose of wireframing your app. Many of these will allow you to create your apps in its most basic form – devoid of color and branding and to iterate often. Whether or not you use available software or decide to go with pen and paper, your wireframes are best refined with feedback from others. So, be sure that you are able to share them and weigh the important feedback. If you need to present your wireframes to a client, then you will want to add a level of polish to your wires. Annotations are also helpful in explaining desired functionality or effects that you may not be able to convey. At the end of your wireframing process, you should be ready to add color, depth, and branding.

Chapter 7

Designing Your Visual Assets with Adobe Photoshop

Adobe Photoshop is probably the most popular graphics software for designers on the planet. When it comes to designing either apps or websites, Adobe Photoshop remains the industry standard. Having been around for over 20 years, it has evolved to become a powerhouse for the creative industry as a whole. The Adobe suite of software programs called Creative Cloud includes other graphics programs such as Adobe Fireworks, Illustrator, InDesign, Premiere Pro, and After Effects and ranges from video editing and image design to motion graphics. For the purpose of this book, however, we will focus on Adobe Photoshop as the standard for creating assets for our iOS application.

I'll touch on Fireworks a little later on, too.

For the purposes of our book and for consistency's sake, we will continue with the theme of our Travel Light app, the app that helps you to never forget what you're taking on a trip. So far we've created an app purpose statement and have done some basic research and wireframes for this fictional application. In this chapter we'll use Photoshop to add some color and branding to the wireframes we've created in Chapter 6. We won't design the app completely from start to finish, but I will show how to complete certain tasks using the software to add color and polish to the user interface of your application.

Some Photoshop Basics

If you've spent most of your time developing apps, you've undoubtedly come into contact with Photoshop files or PSDs as they are commonly referred to. They are the building blocks of most designs. Even if you're only familiar with PNGs (Apple's preferred image format for apps), your PNGs will more likely than not have their humble beginnings as an Adobe Photoshop file.

As this is not a how-to-use Photoshop book, we will assume that we you have some experience with some of the basic tasks in Photoshop. Even as a developer, it is always a good idea to be familiar with Photoshop. Some developers and iOS engineers will receive their PNG assets already sliced and ready for development, while increasingly, some developers are becoming more and more comfortable with receiving the layered PSD files that they will then slice for themselves. This chapter assumes you have some familiarity with Photoshop and have created or edited PSDs before. Ideally, you have opened and explored the UI of the software, created shapes, are familiar with fills, transparency, opacity, and layers, etc.

If you have some experience already, you will be familiar with the layout of Photoshop or as it's referred to by designers, the workspace. That is the screen that you will see upon opening the program and choosing a canvas size for the app you are about to design. Since you will be creating for iOS, your canvas should display the basic outline or shape of an iOS device.

If you are an absolute beginner with Photoshop, do a search for Photoshop tutorials or Photoshop basics. There are tons of online resources for those who are new to design and want to learn the basics of Photoshop. Depending on the amount of time that you have to devote to classes, tutorials, and practice, it is fair to say that you can get up to speed in a matter of weeks. Then, you can return to this chapter in this book and continue. Photoshop is a complex tool, although recent efforts have been made to make it more user friendly. If you've never seen or touched this software program, it can appear to be confusing.

The first step in creating your app in Photoshop will be to start a new document in Photoshop. If you're designing for the iPhone and iOS 7, you're designing for the 4, 4S, 5, 5S, and 5C. If your app is going to be backwards compatible to iOS 6, then the 3GS might be included since iOS 6 still supports this device. However, with adoption rates for iOS 7 being what they are and for the purposes of our app, we're designing for iOS 7.

Because the newer devices have Retina screens, the accepted approach is to design for higher resolution and then scale down for lower resolution devices. This also means that you will need multiple versions of your assets for all of the different versions of the iPhone that currently exist.

Prepping for Retina

Before we get to the business of designing the app, here are some things to consider. Since every iPhone since the iPhone 3GS features a Retina screen, we'll set up our Photoshop file as such. If you're designing for Retina, and you have a new Retina computer such as Apple's MacBook Pro with Retina, then you're all set. These computers will render your Retina designs as they are meant to look on a Retina device. But, don't worry if you don't have a Retina computer. There are other solutions. LiveView is a free app that some designers use. It allows them to view their designs remotely on their mobile devices. It is available for iPhone and iPad and will let you view your Adobe Photoshop canvas in real time, on the iOS device of your choosing. You will have to install the application on your computer and your mobile device for it to work. LiveView works with non-Retina screens, too.

Another tool that helps designers view their designs on mobile devices is Skala. Available for the Mac, iPhone, iPad, and Android, this tool appears to be popular among designers, too. There are other tools available, so do some research before you commit to one. The two mentioned previously are pretty popular and have great support.

Your Photoshop Setup

Setting up your screen in Photoshop is relatively easy. You will need your wireframes for reference. Make a list of the screens you need to create in Photoshop. Based on our wireframes, these are:

1. Loading screen

2. Registration/Sign-in

3. My Trip

4. Edit Trip

5. Select Trip

6. Edit Trip Items

From the list above, we'll create the following screens:

Registration/Sign-in, Trip details (Entry), and Edit Trip Items.

This list for the most part, represents all of the pages we will need to design for our app. We'll skip things like the launch image and assume that it will feature some sort of logo or even be identical to your app's first page. Apple's Human Interface Guidelines aren't fond of launch images that are heavily branded anyway, and users won't really be interacting with that screen or seeing it for a significant amount of time, anyway. However, there is more information on creating launch images in Chapter 8. We'll focus, for now, on the screens that the user will actually be interacting and that represent some level of functionality. The first screen that users will see when they enter the app will be the sign-in or registration screen.

Let's start creating our first screen in Photoshop. It's a good idea to have your wireframes nearby so that you can use them for reference.

The first thing you will need to do is to create a new project in Photoshop. This will be the basis of all of your screens moving forward. Set your dimensions as shown in Figure 7-1.

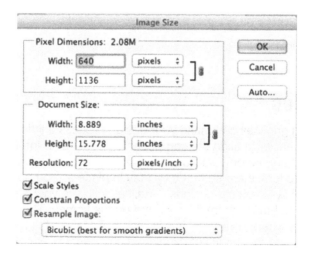

Figure 7-1. Adobe Photoshop's image size window

The 640 x 1196 will accommodate the higher resolution of the newer iPhones, including the recently released iPhone 5c and 5s. Starting at a higher resolution will also make it easier to scale down your assets for non-Retina devices. It's pretty easy to do this once you design for the higher resolution. Once you're set up for this and all of your elements and components have even dimensions, you will then be able to scale down to accommodate non-Retina design for older devices.

After you've set up your canvas in Photoshop, you'll be taken to the main screen where you will proceed to design your app. It will look something like the screenshot in Figure 7-2 depending on your personal preferences. Before you start adding elements and components, take some time to set up some aspects of the canvas, like which panels you prefer to be visible and where you want panels – depending on your orientation – right- or left-handed. Once you have arranged all of the panels and set up the canvas to your liking, this will make your design process easier. Most of Photoshop's panels and windows can be moved around or hidden, according to your preferences.

Figure 7-2. Main canvas in Photoshop

Gridlines & Guides

Setting up and establishing gridlines can make your design process a little easier. Guides and gridlines will make it much easier to align the components in your user interface across multiple screens. They are lines that appear on your page but not in your applications. You can put grids anywhere on the screen and lock them so that they stay in place as you design your app. They will help you to create perfectly symmetrical designs. Gridlines will give your elements exact placement on the canvas as opposed to having them float around on the screen. The alternative is to do this by the naked eye and estimate where components will line up. For even the most professional designer, this can be a tedious affair, and the results of misplaced components are elements that jump around from screen to screen. You will want to make sure that your elements snap to a guide or a grid to ensure that they do not move around from screen to screen. Even a pixel will cause movement if all of the elements have not been perfectly aligned.

Guides are simple lines that appear when you are attempting to align certain elements on your screen. You can set the preferences for your guides by going to **Preferences➤Guides, Grids & Slices**.

There are a few different ways to create a grid and gridlines, and this can get pretty complicated when it comes to gridlines and subdivisions, but we will use the gridlines provided with Photoshop and use them as a guide to keep our components on each screen aligned. You can also check out a selection of Photoshop plug-ins and extensions that are available that help with creating gridlines for everything from websites to apps. For now, we'll keep it simple and get on with the business of designing our Travel Light app.

The main canvas shown in in Figure 7-2 is where you will do most of your work. To the left you will see the Tools panel with the main canvas in the middle. Note the shape of the screen matches the aspect ratio and dimensions of an iPhone screen and the layers panel on the far right. There are a number of ways to customize this screen. Photoshop allows you to only keep elements you find critical on the screen so that you are able to focus on the tasks at hand. I recommend playing around with different combinations to find a layout that works for you. For the purposes of designing our app, however, we'll stick to this screen. I'll describe the panels in further detail next.

The Tools Panel

The Tools panel is pretty much just that. All of the tools available to you in Photoshop will be located in this panel. The panel can be moved pretty much anywhere on the screen you like. But upon initial launch, it will be located to the far left. It is shown in Figure 7-3.

Figure 7-3. The Tools panel in Photoshop

In order to view what each tool in the panel does, hold your pointer over it and the name of the tool will pop up just under it. It's a good idea to do this for all of the tools in the panel so that you are at least familiar with what each tool is called and to get a sense of what it does. To select a tool, simply click on it in the panel. If you see a small triangle in the lower right, that usually means that there are additional options that you can select from within that tool's menu. The organization of the Tools panel follows.

Selection Tools

In the selection section of the Tools panel, you'll find the following tools that allow you to select various shapes:

- Move - Allows you to move a layer or image selection.
- The Marquee Tool - The marquee tool allows the user to make a selection in the shape of the tool (rectangular, elliptical, single column, and single row).

- The Lasso - The lasso tool allows the user to draw a freehand border around a particular selection like you would with a pen or pencil. This tool is also available as polygonal and magnetic tools. The magnetic lasso automatically detects the edge of a selection and the polygonal tool will draw along already-straight lines.

- The Quick Selection Tool – This tool lets you make selections based on color.

- The Magic Wand – The magic wand allows users to make selections in high-contrast images.

Crop and Slice Tools

The Crop and Slice tools allow you to extract a section of an image for your use or to create a series of smaller images from a main image. They include:

- Crop - The crop tool allows you to crop or remove areas of an image.

- Slice - These tools allow users to slice image selections for the Web or other use.

Measuring Tools

Measuring tools in Photoshop allow you to measure between two points in an image. Measuring tools are coupled with some other tools that also include:

- Eyedropper – Allows you to select a particular color for your foreground.

- Color Sampler – Primarily used in color correction, this tool will log a particular color area's color value.

- Ruler – Allows you to measure the distance between two points.

- Note – Allows annotations to be added to an image or document.

Retouching Tools

The Retouching tools allow you to retouch and clean or even delete selected parts or portions of your image that need improvement. Tools in this section include:

- Spot Healing – Allows you to match textures from one image onto another to repair or cover imperfections in an image. Best for imperfections that are round.

- Healing Brush – Allows you to repair image imperfections that aren't round.

- Patch – Repairs imperfections in images by blending two areas.

- Red Eye – Corrects the popular red-eye problem in photographs.

- Clone Stamp – Allows you to cover or to clone one part of an image onto another part of an image.

- Eraser – Allows you to erase unwanted portions of your image.

- Background & Magic Eraser – Allows you to remove unwanted backgrounds from images.

- Blur – Allows you to paint and make a portion of an image blurry.

- Sharpen – Makes an image looks sharper.

- Smudge – Allows you to smear or smudge a selection of an image.

- Dodge – Replicates a photographer's dodging process. This tool lets you lighten part of an image.

- Burn – Cousin of the Dodge tool, this tool allows you to darken parts of an image.

- Sponge – Works to increase or to decrease a color's saturation.

Painting Tools

The Painting tools allow you to paint or to replicate the act of painting with a brush or different types of tools. They allow you to change and customize the brushes to your preference and to choose from a variety of options. Painting tools include:

- Brush – Lets you paint with a brush and a variety of different tips.

- Pencil – Replicates drawing with a pencil.

- Color replacement – Allows you to swap one color for another when painting.

- Mixer Brush – Lets you create painting effects by "mixing" different colors.

- History Brush – Lets you revert to an older version of your work by painting over a selection to reveal the older version.

- Art History Brush – This tool takes the History Brush tool and adds an effect to it.

- Gradient – Lets you create a background or overlay that blends one color into another to create a gradient.

- Paint Bucket – Fills an area with a solid color.

Draw & Type Tools

The Draw and Type tools are for drawing shapes and writing or typing in an image you are creating. Tools in this section include:

- Pen Tool – Lets you click two anchor points and Photoshop will draw a line between them.

- Freeform Pen – Allows you to draw freehand as with a pen.

- Horizontal & Vertical Type – Add text to an image either horizontally left to right or vertically top to bottom.

- Mask Tools – Allow you to create outlines of text.

- Path Selection – Allows you to select a path that has been created by any of the other tools.

- Direct Selection – Allows you to select anchor points or parts of a particular path as opposed to an entire path.

- Shape – Lets you draw a number of different shapes (rectangle, ellipse, polygon, line, or custom shapes).

View and Navigation Tools

The View and Navigation tools allow you to move images around or to zoom in for a different view.

- Hand – Allows you to move images around on the screen.

- Rotate View – Allows you to rotate your particular view of an image.

- Zoom – Allows you to zoom in on an image.

3D Tools

3D tools allow you to manipulate and rotate 3D models in Photoshop. The tools in this section include:

- 3D Object Rotate (Includes object roll, pan, slide, and scale) – Allows you to rotate, manipulate, and scale a 3D model.

- 3D Rotate Camera – Rotates a 3D camera view while leaving the actual 3D object fixed.

The Layers Panel

Assuming you've set up your stage as I did in Figure 7-2, your Layers panel shown in Figure 7-4 will be on your right where you will be able to see all of the elements in your design. You will use this panel to manage the design of your app. When you create your very first image as seen in Figure 7-2, this will most likely be the background of your app. While you can have multiple layers in your design, you can only have one background.

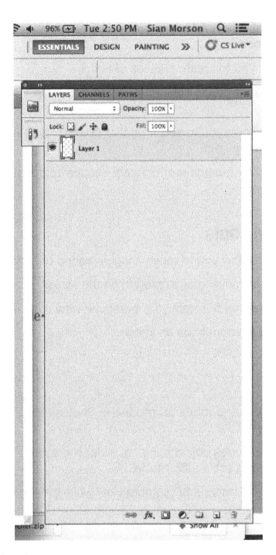

Figure 7-4. The Layers panel in Photoshop

From the Layers panel, you can change preferences and properties for each layer such as transparency and opacity of a given layer.

Layers are building blocks of anything that you create on the Photoshop canvas. If your app is extremely complex, then you will have quite a few layers. Get into the habit of naming your layers and making sure that they follow the natural structure of your application. That is to say, when you open your master files and look at your design, your layers should easily correspond to your design. You will want to give your layers names that correspond to your design.

For example, this makes it easier to make edits and for your developer to find layers. Photoshop will name layers but not in an intuitive way (i.e., layer 1, 2, 3, etc.). If you have a file with a large number of layers, discovering which layer you need to edit if they don't correspond to actual elements in your design will take a significant amount of time. Once they start to add up, you will see that naming them is easiest.

Layers can also be grouped. Thus, if you have a few layers associated with a particular element such as a tab bar, you might want to group those layers or put them into one folder. This makes them easier to find when it comes to development or if you have to make changes later on to your designs.

Whether you are choosing elements from templates you find floating around the Internet – and there are many – or creating your own, make sure that these elements are in vector form. Vectors can be scaled and adjusted to your liking without losing quality. In Photoshop, vectors are called shape layers. You'll see how useful they are when you begin to scale from Retina down to non-Retina.

Creating the Registration/Sign-in Page

For the purposes of our Travel Light app, we will keep the design fairly simple. Our first screen will be the registration or login screen for our app. While simple, this screen is incredibly important. It is the first encounter that your users will have with your app. Therefore, branding colors will need to be apparent on this screen as well, so choose your background color wisely. If you already have a color palette that you're working with, this can save you hours in guesswork and trying out various color combinations. If you know what color you'd like to use for your base color, a simple way to get a palette together is to alter the hue and brightness of your base to create a few variations. To do this, you'll need to open the color picker window in Photoshop. The color picker panel is accessible by clicking any of the color swatches that represent the foreground or background color at the bottom of the Tools panel. From there, you can choose either Hex codes or use the picker to select a color by sight. You will also be able to adjust your saturation or brightness from here. I've shown the color picker below in Figure 7-5.

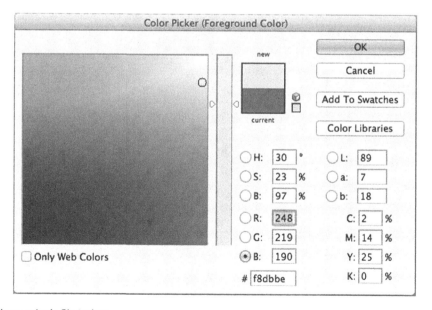

Figure 7-5. Picking a color in Photoshop

For the purposes of our Travel Light app, we've chosen a very pastel-inspired color palette. Note the settings in the screenshot above. We'll use this as the background and the other as the foreground of our Travel Light application.

Once our background is in, we'll label the background as such and lock it so that we are able to move freely around on top of that layer. You don't want it moving too much as you position your elements. Then, use the shape tool to draw the shapes that will represent your entry fields (both e-mail login and password) as well as the submit button.

You don't want to overwhelm them with too much information here. Your goal is to collect their info and get them into the app as fast as possible. Make it simple. The first order of business will be for users to know how they can access the app. Going from our wireframes, we are creating a simple registration page that allows the user to enter his or her e-mail address and a password and then submit that information to access the app.

The screens in Figure 7-6 represent the designed page with gridlines and one without. You can work with or without them. You can turn them on or off by using the following path: View➤Snap To. You are able to see how the gridlines help to align all of the elements on the screen. The screen in Figure 7-7 shows the entire canvas including the Tools menu so that you can see how I've named the layers corresponding to this page.

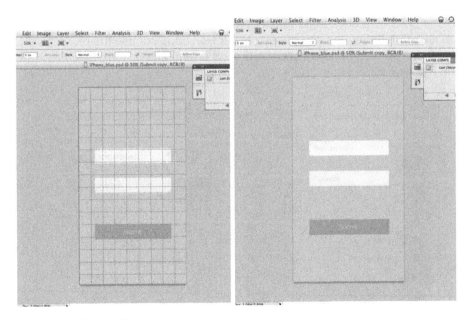

Figure 7-6. Sign-in screen with and without gridlines

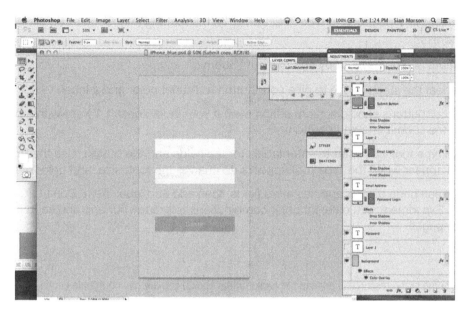

Figure 7-7. *Travel Light sign-in screen canvas*

We've just created our first page for the Travel Light app primarily by using the rectangle tool to create two fields and a button. Here are the steps I took after setting up the stage and creating the background:

To create the e-mail and password fields:

1. Create a new layer and call it "Email address."

2. Use the rectangle tool to draw a rectangle that will represent the e-mail address field. The gridlines will help you to ensure that the field is the appropriate width and if you have your smart guides turned on, they will help you to center it on the screen.

3. Use the guides to help you vertically align the e-mail field slightly higher on the screen, leaving room for the second field.

4. Select a color for the field and name the layer "Email."

5. Select the type tool and type "Email address" in the rectangle.

6. Adjust the size of the font and color if you need to.

7. Copy the layer by right clicking and selecting "Duplicate layer" from the menu. Photoshop will create a new layer called "Email address copy."

8. Double click on the title to change it to "Password."

9. Use the Move tool to move the new field. Position it slightly below, ensuring that it is aligned with the one above.

10. Select the Type tool and type "Password" in the rectangle to replace "Email address."

11. Create another layer copy and name it "Submit."

12. Repeat the steps above to give your button a distinct color and a label.

The color of your buttons should scream action even if your label doesn't. I went with a bright green (#12e30d) for the submit or sign-in button.

The horizontal type tool was used to enter labels for the fields and the button. Use the Properties panel that will appear when the Type tool appears, to change the font, size, and color of the type.

If the home screen page of your app has more fields, then add and label them. Don't forget to add an action button. Experiment with different color combinations to brand your app and keep it consistent with the lower pages.

> **Tip**   Use some of the resources I pointed out earlier in the book if you are having trouble coming up with a color scheme for your app.

Creating the Select and Edit Trips Page

Now, let's move onto a page with more elements.

The next page we'll focus on will be the "Select Trip" and "Edit Trips" pages. This is the page that will allow users who have already entered their trips to select them from a list view in the app. From a user experience standpoint, the assumption here is that a user has already entered the details for his or her frequent trips into the app. So, the next screen he or she will logically see would be a screen that shows a list of his or her trips. From that screen, a user should be able to drill down to see the details of each trip or to edit his or her list of trips. We will create both pages.

Starting with a blank canvas, fill the screen with the background color much like we did for the sign-in/registration screen. The sign-in page we created in Figures 7-5 and 7-6 are actually missing the status bar, so we will add it to this screen and all subsequent screens. iOS 7 allows you to customize the status bar, so it's possible to make it transparent so that the color of the nav bar will show through. Subsequent pages will have the status bar as users will want to see the status, and it is a usability best practice to keep it visible except in rare cases. Since this is a productivity app, I've decided to keep the status bar visible once the user has moved past the registration page.

You will note that the My Trips page is a simple page with a map on top and a list of trips below for the user to choose from.

I created this page by grabbing a few elements from Applidium's iOS 7 template in PSD format. The template has lots of the new UI elements featured in iOS 7 and it is possible to simply grab a layer from the template PSD and add it to the current work. For the designs in Figure 7-8, I imported the compose button on the My Trips page and the controls to the left of each trip on the Edit Trips page. To do this, select the layer and right click to reveal additional options. Then, select merge layers and choose the name of the current file you are working on to add the set of layer to your current canvas.

Merging the layers will make them uneditable once imported. So unless you are planning to use a set of layers or a layer in the form it appears with no editing, it's a good idea to select the group of layers and import them without merging.

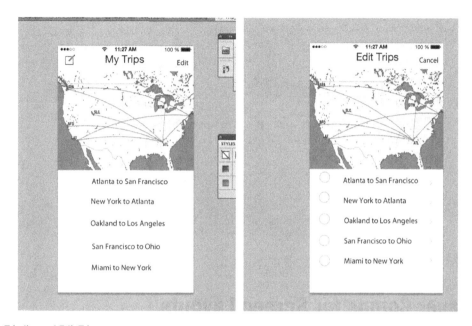

Figure 7-8. Trip list and Edit Trips screens

Once your layer is imported, you should be able to work with it in your current document. If you've converted it to a smart object, this should be easy as you can now resize to suit your design.

Note   A smart object is a file that has data from a raster or vector image in it. It allows users to edit the file while saving its source content.

I imported the map image from a general google search and this is just for illustration only. The arrows to the right of each item in the table view were imported directly from the template. Selecting any item in the trips menu will take the user to the detailed view of that page. I've created a page for the Miami to New York trip to show how this would look. As this page is visually not too different from the previous parent page, I used the previous page as a template for the following pages in Figure 7-9 and changed the menu items. Much like the My Trips page, the "Edit" button in the upper right corner of the screen will bring up the deletion controls in each cell of the table view. These items will be added programmatically but I added them into the designs for your reference in the Edit Trip Items screen. Hitting the cancel button will take the user back to the Main Miami to New York Trip page. The controls to the left of each menu item were imported from the Applidium iOS 7 PSD.

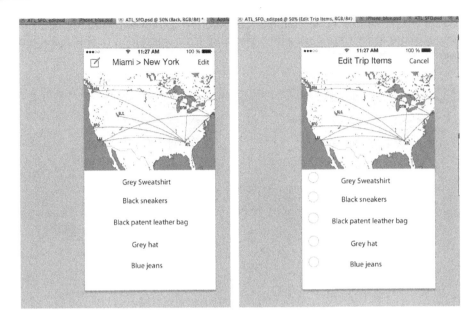

Figure 7-9. Item list and Item edit screens

Using Layer Comps for Screen Layouts

Layer comps are a great tool to use to lay out your various versions of the screens for your iPhone app. Layer comps allow you to save the visibility, position, and appearance of a design once you complete it. They are a great tool for designers because they removes the need to remember all of the different styles that you apply to a specific design or save each one as aseparate PSD file with multiple layers. As you may or may not know, PSD files with multiple layers can get pretty large. It is also a feature that you will find handy if you are creating multiple variations on a design or screen and need to present them to a client for review. A layer comp is pretty easy to create.

1. From the Windows menu at the top of the canvas in Photoshop, scroll down and choose the Layer Comps option. It will open up the layer comps window.

2. From that window, select the new layer icon at the bottom of the window. The screenshot in Figure 7-9 shows a window with our design, the layer comp window as well as the pointer hovering over the "New Layer comp" icon.

3. After each variation on the design has been completed, click the new layer comp icon. It will open a pop-up window that will allow you to enter a name for the comp.

4. You will also have the option of saving the visibility, position or appearance (layer style) of the design. Check any or all that apply and add any comments or notes that you need and click OK. You've saved your layer comp.

Any additional changes can be saved as a layer comp in the exact same way.

When you've finalized which styles of layers work for you and you are ready for development, layer comps can be easily exported to the file format of your choice for review or each comp can be exported as a separate PSD if that is a requirement. This can be done by choosing File➤Scripts➤Layer Comps to Files as shown in Figure 7-10.

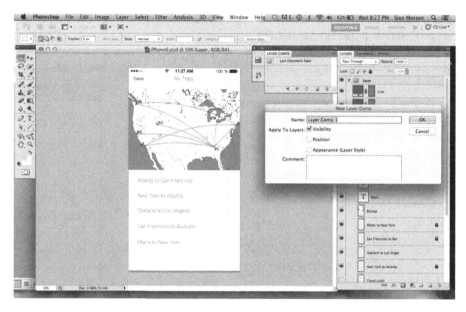

Figure 7-10. *Creating a layer comp*

What about Adobe Fireworks?

There are some in the design community who might be asked the above question right now. Some designers are passionate supporters and fans of Adobe Fireworks, another graphics software tool that is a part of Adobe's Creative Suite. Recently, however (May 2013 to be exact), Adobe announced that it will not be adding new features to Fireworks. While it will continue to include Fireworks in Adobe Creative Suite 6, and Creative Cloud as well as sell it, they will no longer be devoting engineering time or talent in making improvements or additional upgrades to the software. Adobe, will, however, continue to support the software. That being said, Fireworks is a worthy, yet simpler alternative to Photoshop for creating your designs for your iOS app. Fireworks is structured in a similar way to Photoshop and the user interface is similar. As you can see in the screenshot below, if you're familiar with the Photoshop Interface, then Fireworks will be strikingly familiar. The screenshots below is a Photoshop PSD of our Travel Light app's screen details page in Fireworks. One of the great things about Fireworks is that is reads and writes PSD files as well as other graphic formats.

Adobe Fireworks has a great reputation as an awesome tool for prototyping and exporting. So, if you've created your design in Photoshop and need to slice and export them as PNGs then Fireworks will assist with that nicely and be sure that your exports will be ready for use in Xcode.

Another advantage of using Adobe Fireworks is that any object you create is in vector format. That will help greatly when you will need to scale your assets down or up for any reason (and you will need to scale down for older versions of the iPhone). You will find that this applies to effects and filters, too. This may not be such a huge issue as flat design has done away with some heavy usage of effects, but it will come in handy if you need to use them and if so, they are better uses and will scale easily in Fireworks.

If we import our PSD from Figure 7-11 into Fireworks, we can continue to edit it much as we would in Photoshop. The interface for Fireworks is slightly less complicated in my humble opinion, and it's a little more user friendly. So, you can either complete your designs in Fireworks or create your entre design in either program and get similar results.

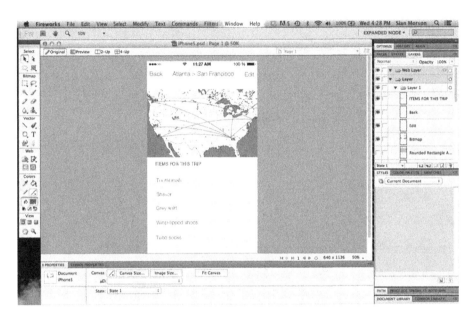

Figure 7-11. Trip List PSD in Adobe Fireworks

With the techniques outlined in this chapter, you should be able to create a simple design for iOS. You won't be a seasons iPhone designer, but with a bit of practice and just using the processes I used above, you should be able to create most of the pages in the app.

Summary

Adobe Photoshop is the de facto standard for digital design today. Arguably, this graphics program is at the root of every app design. In order to design apps, you will need to learn how to use Photoshop. Its lesser-used cousin, Adobe Fireworks works, too but will no longer be supported by Adobe. If you're going to be taken seriously as s designer, you will need to become fluent in Photoshop. Both Photoshop and Fireworks are great tools for designing your app. Your PSDs can work in both programs, too, if you decide that one is easier to use. Both are by Adobe and feature various tools to make the design process easier. Exploring the Tools panel will help you to familiarize yourself with the tools you need to create the interface of your app. The other panel that you will need to pay attention to is the Layers panel. Be sure to name your layers in an intuitive way because it is likely that your design will generate numerous layers. Layer comps are useful if you are creating multiple screens or different versions of your app to show your client.

Chapter 8

Creating Your App Icon and Additional Graphics for the App Store

By this time, you've almost completed the entire process of designing your application and have handed it off to your developer for development. While you can add the app icon to the bundle with your other assets for development, the app icon is something that you can focus on independently. As a rule, your app should have some level of polish to it.

Though we've discussed icons before as they relate to other areas in your app such as the tab bar and UI, I've created this chapter to focus exclusively on icons and the other graphics that need to be included in your app bundle that you will eventually deliver to Apple. As we are aware, Apple places a high premium on aesthetic design. It is fair to say that your apps should not only adhere to the UI standards set forth in the Human Interface Guidelines, but they should also be beautiful. The strict guidelines placed on app design are there for a reason. Those guidelines extend to the design of your app's icon as well, and the app's icon is the main way that users will discover your app in the app store. It is used in a number of different locations in the app store. In this chapter, I'll talk about the other graphics that are required for your iOS app. These include promotional artwork, your app icons, screenshots, and your app's page in the app store. If your app is a magazine app, then this will include the newsstand icon as well. These are used to showcase your app to potential customers. A well-designed icon and well-chosen screenshots for your app can mean the difference between a potential customer downloading your app and passing it by.

App Discovery

The app discovery process is quite simple. A user has a few ways of finding out about your app. He or she may read about your app in an article if you are lucky enough to get press coverage, or in one of the many app review sites like 148Apps, Appolicious, or AppCraver. These sites keep track of new releases and offer in-depth reviews of apps in virtually every category available. The sites are helpful if you want to find out information on an app before downloading, based on certain criteria. These sites are popular and often have loyal followings. They are also great because they provide information on price drops.

> **TIP** Developers will sometimes offer special promotions on paid apps and lower the price of purchase for a period of time. These promotions are called price drops and can begin and end without warning.

While review sites and articles are great for finding out about new apps, perhaps one of the most tried and true ways of discovering apps is simply by browsing Apple's own app store.

The App Store

The app store is more than just a store. It is actually a digital distribution platform for the iOS apps. While the term "app store" can now also be applied to the Mac app store as well, for the purposes of this book, we will focus on the iOS app store. The app store distributes apps for all iOS devices and is the primary outlet for users to purchase and download iOS applications.

The app store app is included and preinstalled on every iOS device. The app connects users directly to the store and facilitates their purchases of apps. It is also connected to iTunes Connect and a user's iTunes account.

> **Tip** iTunes Connect is a web portal for iOS developers. It allows them to manage different versions of their apps, reports, and all metadata associated with their apps.

As you know, a user must have an iTunes account in order to purchase apps on his or her device. iTunes and your Apple ID will allow you to access iTunes Connect and submit your app to Apple for review and then distribution in the app store. Users will be able to download your app directly to their devices via the app store app. The app store's app is included on every iOS device and is recognizable via its unique icon, which features a paintbrush, pencil, and ruler arranged in an "A" formation. The newly revised flat logo is shown in Figure 8-1.

Figure 8-1. *The app store icon's new look for iOS 7*

The app store is responsible for 50 billion app downloads and 575 million store accounts. Sorting through all of them can take up some time. As the number of apps in the store increased, Apple has made subtle improvements to the app store's navigability over the years. Categories like Editor's Choice have been added, Featured apps are displayed more prominently, Collections of apps have been grouped together, and it is even possible to find holiday-themed apps like those for Halloween or Christmas in the app store. Most recently, a category of apps have been added specifically designed for iOS 7. Since its release, this selection of apps has been prominently displayed in the app store.

All apps that have been submitted and approved by Apple for distribution will appear in the app store.

To submit your app to the app store, you will need the following assets:

- App icon
- Launch image
- Newsstand cover icon (if app falls in that category)
- Screenshots
- Promotional artwork

The app icon, launch images, and newsstand cover icons are included in the app bundle, which is a package created by Xcode that includes your app executable and all supporting resources including app icons, image files, and content.

The App Icon

The app icon is the first thing users will see that will be representative of your application. It will represent your app on a device's home screen as well as in the app store. The app icon is required, and apps submitted without it will be rejected. While some of the icons and artwork mentioned in the Human Interface Guidelines are optional, the app icon is not.

If you're creating a new app to submit to the app store, then you should refer to the Human Interface Guidelines for the latest dimensions and requirements for app icons for all devices as well as Spotlight search results and Settings icon.

You may think that because of their size, app icons offer little room for originality or creativity. You would be wrong. There are entire sites and galleries dedicated to beautifully designed app icons and sites like Dribbble and Behance where designers and creative from all fields post-concept and real-life designs for app icons. Study and review some designs for inspiration for your app's icons. Aside from the dimensions, your app's icon must help to visually convey to potential users exactly what your app is about while encompassing additional bits of information like branding where possible. Your choice of colors, as with your application, will speak to users, too. So, they must be chosen wisely. Your app icon must be unique in that it must stand out among a sea of other apps vying for potential users' attention. You can drill down to the section of the app store that features apps specifically designed for iOS 7 and look closely at some of those icons. Some of them may be able to inspire you in the design of your app icon.

There are a number of guidelines that Apple provides for designing app icons. Here are the Do's and Don'ts directly from the Human Interface Guidelines.

Do:

- If possible, get help from a professional graphic designer
- Make sure your user easily recognizes images
- Keep it simple and devoid of words
- Test it against a variety of backgrounds
- Avoid transparency
- Make sure it scales well and is legible at all sizes

Don't:

- Use iOS or Apple elements
- Use any Apple imagery at all

The new shape of the app icon in iOS 7 compared to that of iOS 6 is subtle. To the naked eye, one may or may not notice the difference in the corner radius of the icon. And honestly, for designers, this isn't a huge deal as iOS will add a mask that applies the rounded effect to app icons automatically. However, there has been much speculation about the new design of the iOS 7 app icon. Mathematical formulas have been written, and there has been much speculation on the meaning behind the new icon. What's most important at this juncture for any designer is making sure that the icon is conveying the message that it needs to for users. The app icon must also look its best on a number of different back grounds and at the various different sizes that are required.

Launch Images

The launch image is an image that iOS displays when your app starts up. You will have to include at least one launch image in your app bundle. Users of your app will only see the launch image briefly before they actually begin to interact with your app. Think of it this way: if your app launches quickly, the launch image will flash on the device's screen and then take the user directly into your app. If your app takes longer to load, then users will see it for longer. If you think of it that way, then you will be able to conceive of a better launch image for your app. If you were a user, what would you want to see before you enter the app? Apple also recommends staying away from any sort of welcome verbiage or introduction, or an about page on the launch image.

Some designers have even made their launch image identical to the initial page of their application. This gives the appearance that the app has loaded quickly and is a practice that some designers and developers use as well.

Apple, in the Human Interface Guidelines, recommends making a launch screen that is identical to the initial page of an application without text or UI elements. This way, when your app actually loads there is no jarring visual transition between the launch image and your app.

Last, all launch images must include the status bar regions. Launch image size recommendations are listed in Table 8-1.

Table 8-1. Launch Image Sizes for All Devices

Device	Size
For iPhone 5 series (iPhone & iPod touch)	640 x 1136 px
For iPhone and iPod touch	640 x 960 px
	320 x 480 px (standard resolution)
iPad Portrait	1536 x 2048 px
	768 x 1024 px (standard resolution)
iPad Landscape	2048 x 1536 px
	1024 x 768 px (standard resolution)

Newsstand Cover Icon

If your app falls into the newsstand category, there are specific rules for its icon. Your icon will be displayed in the newsstand app along with other magazines and publications. Because of the way these apps are displayed, Apple has created different rules for these icons. Your newsstand cover icon is separate from the app icon so be sure not to confuse the two. The newsstand cover icon should be a replica of the cover of an issue of your actual magazine or periodical. It identifies your app in the newsstand app while your app icon will generally identify the app in the app store. Keep the newsstand icon general and not too specific, but remember that you definitely want users to see the cover and identify your magazine with it. So, keep the font and layout consistent with what regular readers of the magazine to expect, but leave out any seasonal or issue-specific details. Figure 8-2 shows that app icon and the newsstand icons look like and also shows how they are different.

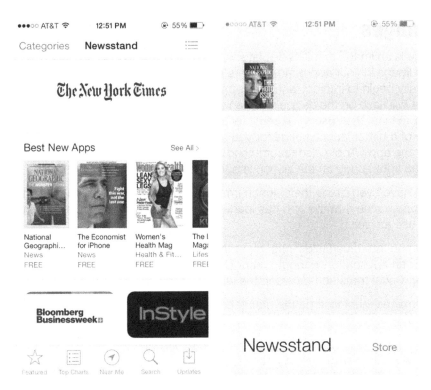

Figure 8-2. *The newsstand section on the app store and an app on the iPhone*

Refer to the Human Interface Guidelines for specific instructions, as there are specific sizes and aspect ratio requirements that will need to be adhered to.

Along with your default cover icon you will need to include a separate issue icon that acts as a visual representation of each new issue as it appears not only on the newsstand "shelf" but also in the multitasking bar on various devices. This icon, unlike the default cover, can include some specific details about the content of that issue so that users are able to identify it. As with other icons, do not add any visual embellishments or enhancements to newsstand icons. The addition of enhancements in appearance such as corners, pages, or perspective is specifically forbidden.

Promotional Screenshots

Screenshots of your app are an important part of your promotion in the Apple app store. Screenshots are displayed on your app's page along with metadata, a description, and your app's icon. Screenshots aren't a part of your app's bundle, but at least one is required when submitting your app via iTunes Connect. If you can only include one screenshot of the app, make it the best one. While only one screenshot is absolutely required with your bundle for the submission and acceptance to the app store, I recommend that you add as many as Apple will allow, which was five last time I checked. Five screenshots are plenty and with those you can really give users a sense of what the interface of your app is like and what they can expect when they download it.

Also, the order of your screenshots will matter. They will be displayed in the order in which they are uploaded so a sequential view of the user interaction of your app is a nice way to orient users to your app and its most important or exciting features. Screenshots also will go a long way toward increasing the discoverability of your app in the app store. If your app only has one screenshot (as required), users won't be able to get a good sense of your app's interface. In this day and age when so many apps are pushing the boundaries of design, adding as many screenshots as possible gives users a sense of what they will be getting for the time and money (if your app isn't free) that they will invest in downloading your app.

If your app is visually unique or contains an innovative feature, you can also include a screenshot of this page or feature. If the app is a universal app and will run on an iPad, you are required to add a screenshot of your app on the iPhone *and* iPad along with your app submission.

Your screenshots should be high quality files and the visuals should be clear and crisp. Apple documentation states that if you take screenshots from an actual device running your app, that the status bar should be removed before uploading them. However, a quick scan of the app store shows quite a few apps with screenshots including the status bar. It seems as though this is not an offense that will cause your app to be rejected from the app store. The app store will, however, only accept screenshots in the following formats: JPEG, TIFF, or PNG. Figure 8-3 shows two screenshots from the Travel Light app with and without the status bar.

Figure 8-3. The image on the right is acceptable for submission to the app store. The one on the left is not

Users of iOS devices are familiar with the manual way of creating screenshots, which is to hold the home and power buttons. If you are familiar with Xcode and have a version of your app that you can compile and run, you can also take screenshots that way. These screenshots will be permissible for the app store as well.

Here's a list of Do's and Don'ts for your screenshots.

Do:

- Make sure your content is legible in all sizes
- Upload the maximum number of screenshots (5) for your app
- Use your devices to take screenshots of your app
- Remove the status bar from all screenshots
- Think about how your app's images will translate across country and cultural borders
- Localize screenshots if necessary

Don't:

- Add marketing messages to your screenshots
- Include a device frame around the image

Promotional Artwork

If your app is exceptional in execution and design, Apple may decide to feature it in the app store. If you feel that your app might be chosen by Apple to be featured or think that your app has a good chance, then it's a good idea to create promotional artwork assets ahead of time. Even if you don't think your app stands a chance, it's a good idea to get into the habit of creating promotional artwork for your app. Promotional artwork lets you add a little creativity into your images to give users a visual story behind your apps. But Apple will have the final say on what this looks like once it has been added to the app store.

Unless you have some prior knowledge of this (which is rare) the request will be unexpected and will usually have a time deadline associated with it. So, better safe than sorry or safe than scrambling.

While there is no tried and true formula for what Apple will feature in the app store, it's a safe bet to say that your app must be well designed and have a unique look and feel to be featured in the app store. If your app has lots of downloads and is incredibly popular, that can sometimes help. But mostly, Apple looks for apps that really compelling in form and function. Your app must stand on its own and elevate the platform. The app icon is a big part of getting your app noticed by Apple, too. The Human Interface Guidelines specifically state that in order to be considered for a feature, your icons should be original *and* attractive.

Take a look at what's currently featured from week to week and try to get a sense of what's popular. Also note how Apple promotes various apps and how these promotional areas appear in the app store. It is possible that Apple may feature your app in a category with other similar apps or in multiple areas in the app store.

If you get a request for promotional material, it's a good indication that your app will be featured but Apple is clear with the verbiage that this isn't a guarantee of anything. What they are clear about is precisely what they expect to receive from the app creator or owner when such a request is made.

Since Apple's own team will be creating the files they need, they require you to send the layered PSD files. Each PSD file must have a separate layer for all of the various elements. If there are elements that must stay together, then keeping them in a single layer is a good idea. You won't be consulted by Apple's design team on any changes they make to your files if your app is chosen for the app store. So, keeping elements that must stay together in an already flattened layer is a good indicator of what can be moved and what shouldn't. As with everything else that must be submitted to Apple, it must adhere to strict guidelines, and promotional images are no different. Here are some of the specifications for promotional artwork:

- Any background art should be at least 3200 px wide and 600 px high with a minimum of 72 dpi. Background art should also be RGB color and in PSD format only.

- Your artwork should not include text or logos in the Tag area. This is used exclusively for iTunes-related tags. The tag area itself is 200 px from the bottom of the artwork.

- Any text or logos should only appear in the center of artwork in the text/logo safe area.

- Title treatment should be 2004 px wide and 586 px high.

Your App's Page

When your app is ready for submitting to the app store, you will be required to fill in information about your app for your app's page in the app store. Here is the information you'll need to provide:

- Your app's name
- Category
- Rating (Not user rating but ratings for targeted age group)
- Description
- Keywords
- Screenshots
- Supporting URL
- Marketing URL (optional)
- Privacy Policy (optional)
- Contact Info

If your app is a game, has in-app purchases, uses iAds, or includes rights and pricing, you will be required to fill in additional information.

When your app is submitted to the app store and accepted, it is given its very own page and URL. When Apple has approved your app, you will receive an e-mail notifying you that your app is ready for sale with pertinent information about your app. A sample letter I received is shown in Figure 8-4. The e-mail will contain your app ID as well as a link to your app's page in the app store if it is live. Your app's unique ID is a part of the URL. The link will take you to your page where you will see the following:

▓ A large icon of your app

▓ Description of your app's features

▓ Screenshots

▓ Information on the seller

▓ User ratings and reviews

▓ Localized screenshots if necessary

Figure 8-4. Ready for sale e-mail from Apple once an app is approved

Tip   If the app is registered via your developer account, you will receive e-mail notifications from Apple at every stage of the app review process.

If your app has not been approved, you will also receive an e-mail from Apple stating that fact as well as steps you may take to appeal your app's rejection.

Summary

While the design of your app and its user interface is important for your users, when it comes to marketing your app and its place in the Apple app store, your app icon and other graphics that are required are just as important. Apple provides guidelines for creating your app icons, promotional artwork, and screenshots, which all will live on your app's page in the app store once it's approved. It's a good idea to keep these ancillary graphics in the back of your mind as your develop your app's design as they can mean the difference between a download or a quick swipe past in the app store.

Chapter 9

Finalizing Your Assets for App Development

After completing the previous chapter, you should have designed all of the needed pages and screens for your application and created them in such a way that your layers are grouped and named appropriately. If you're lucky, you will also have received feedback or approval from all necessary parties and stakeholders, and can move on with the development of your app. You should, by now, have a clear idea of precisely how users should be interacting with your app, too. All that's needed now is to prep those assets for your developer.

If you've followed the directions in this book from the beginning, you're pretty much ready to complete the process. The hardest part of the application design process is complete, and you're now ready to hand off your designs for development. This, too, is a process with its own set of steps to follow. If you're familiar to some degree with this process, or if you have performed some of these tasks before, you may not find this as tedious as some designers do.

The major tasks include:

- Creating a design specifications document for your developer
- Slicing your designs into assets
- Saving your assets to multiple scales for various devices
- Naming your assets
- Packaging your assets for development

Some developers are familiar with Photoshop and can slice their own assets. If you're a developer, which some of you will be, you may or may not be familiar with Photoshop and how to export your images for iOS development in Xcode. This book and chapter will assume that you will need to slice all of the elements in your screens for your developer. I will not discuss how to prepare assets in Xcode, however.

Creating a Design Specifications Document for Your Developer

If you're handing off your assets to a developer, it is always a great idea to create a reference document or specifications document that will contain everything your developer needs to know before he or she can begin to develop your app. The document should err on the side of providing more information than might be necessary and should also be as unambiguous as possible.

Sometimes, what appears to be straightforward to designers' eyes isn't as simple to developers. A design specifications document can sometimes be as simple as an e-mail or a separate document altogether, but it is a necessary part of the process and will go a long way toward making sure that your app looks and behaves as it should. The design specifications document is delivered along with the final assets for the app. It is also a good practice to review the design specifications document with your developer face-to-face, too, to see if there are any clarifications needed. I'll discuss this in more detail later in the "Communication is Key" section of this chapter.

Design Specifications Document Overview

Start off your document with an overview of the project, the app, and its intended use. This doesn't need to be in great detail; a sentence or two should suffice. If necessary, this can be pulled from the final version of your initial app statement. The overview statement is helpful if you are working with a developer or team of developers who have not been involved in the design and ideation of the app. By providing an overview, you are giving your developer much needed insight into the intended audience for the application and how it will be used.

Your spec document should then guide your developer through the nuances of your application, screen by screen and from beginning to end. As the designer, you will want to pay particular attention to screens that feature effects or that may require unique animations or actions that cannot be shown by your designs. Use annotations liberally in your document if you need to explain how a particular screen should work. Annotations are also incredibly helpful in describing transitions.

Provide Color Information

The document should also contain any clarifications necessary about colors, shades, or hues used throughout the app. Provide color codes where you can, as this is the most precise color information you can provide for a developer. You do not want a developer to guess the colors in your application or have to dig through layers of your PSD (Photoshop document) to find the exact shade.

Specify Fonts & Types

Information regarding fonts and types used in the application should be in the design spec document, too. A developer will need to know the name of the font (even if it is an iOS system font). It will also be important for the developer to know the size of fonts being used in various screens in the app. While Helvetica Neue is the default font for iOS there are many other fonts that are also supported. Sites like iOSfonts.com lists fonts that are supported in iOS, but it's always best to go directly to the source and review Apple's font list to be sure. Apple provides font lists for both iOS 6 and iOS 7. The lists contain all fonts that are installed with both versions of the OS as well as a list of fonts that can be downloaded by apps if necessary.

Tip   A system font is the default font used to display text in menu settings and labels on the iPhone or other iOS device. iOS 7 allows users to change their system fonts.

Explain User Interaction

If needed, add any details about user interaction that need to be clarified. For instance, if one screen of your app contains multiple controllers and will require a variety of different gestures, these will need to be outlined in your design spec. It should let your developer know what user interaction (if not immediately apparent) should yield specific results within your app.

A well-written specifications document will make for an easier transition from design and ideation development, and your initial look or alpha version of the app will appear and behave more like you expect it to.

I've included an example of a page from a design specification document in Figure 8-1. Some clarifications you might want to make in your design specifications document are:

- Buttons that have an on and off state and what they are

- Titles and colors of all buttons (text and type should be removed from buttons before delivering to developer)

- Specific fonts, sizes, and colors to use in specific areas

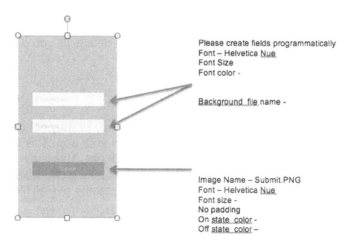

Figure 8-1. Example login/signup page from our Travel Light Design Specifications document

The example page show in Figure 8-1 is quite simple but can easily become more complicated depending on how much detail is added and how complicated your app will be. Ideally, your design specifications document should provide instructions for every screen of your app. Even though they sometimes come in the form of an e-mail, it is a good and well-accepted practice to include the design spec document in the package with your assets that you will deliver to your designer.

If you're developing your own app, it is still a good practice to get into the habit of creating such a document. If you ever need to hand off assets, you'll be ready, and your developer will appreciate it. Contrary to popular belief, your developers want as many details as possible. It helps to inform the task of building the app the way that the creator, client, and ultimately users expect.

Buttons

All iOS apps will have buttons. They are the primary way that users will be interacting with the application. Anything that is tapped or pressed can be considered a button and all buttons have states. The "on" or highlighted state of a button is what the user will see when a button is tapped or interacted with. The "off" or normal state is the state that a user will usually see a button in before they interact with it. A third state is sometimes used, too. That is the inactive state. This means that a button might be shown on a screen but in this state, is not available to the user. As discussed before, buttons in iOS 7 are borderless but they still maintain the properties that most buttons do. This means that unless they are system buttons, they will still need their states to be designed and provided for development.

When preparing buttons for export, all of the assets must be the same size with the exception of their states. This makes for a more seamless interaction in your app. At the very least, your final export of your button(s) should include all applicable states, the sizes in pixels of the font and color, and anything else that applies to that particular asset. If it appears elsewhere in the application but looks (or even behaves) differently, then it is your responsibility to explain these differences so that your developer is aware.

Some buttons can be created programmatically. If you intend for your developer to create a button using Xcode, the same rules apply. Your developer will need to know the exact size of the button, the label, text or font size, and color and exactly how the button is supposed to behave when a user interacts with it.

After your Design Specification Document is complete, review it with your developer to clarify any ambiguities that remain. While your document may contain as many details as you can cram into it, sometimes, nothing beats a face-to-face conversation.

Button Titles

There are a number of ways for developers to create buttons. They may or may not use your provided button asset to create the button that eventually appears in your app. This will usually depend on a few things like whether or not a button has a gradient or not. This is where a conversation with your developer comes in handy. A developer might take a one-pixel section of a graphic and repeat it programmatically to create a button. This reduces the overall file size of the asset and thus your app bundle.

It is a best practice to remove titles from button assets before delivering to your developer. Unless a font cannot be reproduced programmatically, simply provide the graphic(s) and provide detailed instructions in your Design Specifications Document as to what title, font, font size, and color should be associated with the button.

Fonts, Sizes, File Names, and Colors

Your Design Specifications Document should also be a quick reference guide for your developer if there are any questions regarding font names, font sizes, and colors for your buttons Organize your document in a way that is intuitive for you and your developer and make everything easily accessible. A good best practice would be to include actual screens of your app with buttons appearing how they would in the app with a legend on the page that will provide all pertinent information on all elements on that screen:

- Asset file name or names (for all states)
- Font name
- Font size
- Hex code or color
- Location on the screen
- Any specific actions or animations that need to accompany this asset

Slicing Your Designs into Assets

Slicing your assets for delivery to your developer is one of the most important tasks in the asset finalization process. Here, you are slicing up your PSD layer by layer to create individual files of all of the elements that will live within your application. Each element must be sliced to create a unique asset that will be saved as a separate file. Attention to detail becomes critical in this stage of the process.

A critical part of the asset finalization process is also scaling (see the next section). If you remember, we started our design at 1136 x 640 to accommodate for Retina screens for the iPhone 5, 5c, and 5s. If your app is meant to run on all of the different devices supported by iOS, then you will need to provide different sets of assets for each device. This will include the iPhone 4 and 4s. While these two devices have Retina screens, their dimensions differ from that of the newer devices.

The great thing about iOS, however, is that if your app is meant to run on all of these devices, the developer can include all of these assets in one app bundle, and the OS will automatically reference the appropriate file for display on the appropriate device. Assets for Retina screens and devices need to have @2x appended to the root of the file name. I'll talk more about naming conventions later, but this is a standard.

Every designer will have his or her favorite way to slice images and this is usually based on personal preference.

In this chapter I speak explicitly about each step in the slicing and scaling process. My own personal steps for exporting assets for Retina is:

- Select layers (all states)
- Convert to Smart Object
- Save as PNG-24
- Name with @2x

For non-Retina assets the process is as follows:

- Open Retina Smart Object
- Change resolution and scale down to half the size
- Save as PNG-24
- Name WITHOUT @2x

If the process outlined below does not work for you, then experiment within Photoshop to find a way that suits your workflow and accommodates your needs. To slice your asset:

1. Open up the PSD that you will be working on.

2. Choose which asset you want to slice first and then select all of the layers associated with that asset, including all of the states (on, off, etc.) and effects, if it happens to be an action item such as a button.

For illustrative purposes, I've chosen the Submit button from the Travel Light app as an example asset that I will be slicing. As this is a button, we will need to have an on and off state for it. This means that when the user will be interacting with this element, its appearance should change or give the user visual confirmation that action is taking place. Make sure to select all appropriate layers.

3. To select multiple layers, you will need to hold down the "Command" button on your keyboard (Mac) while selecting the layers you need with your mouse or keypad.

The layers should be highlighted as you select them as shown in Figure 8-2.

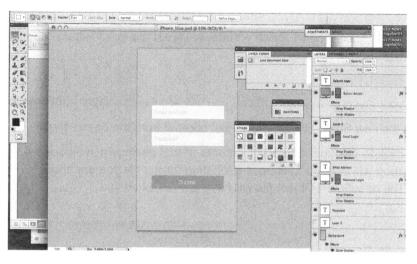

Figure 8-2. *Holding down the Command key allows you to select multiple layers for your asset*

Tip   If a button is used on multiple screens in your app, then remove the type and simply annotate everywhere it is used in your Design Spec doc. For each instance or use of the button, you must also specify the right font, size, and color of the copy for that button. This can be accomplished programmatically and save time.

4.   Now that you've selected your layers, convert them into Smart Objects as I've done in Figure 8-3 by going to Layers ➤ Smart Object. Smart Objects are layers that contain data from vector images.

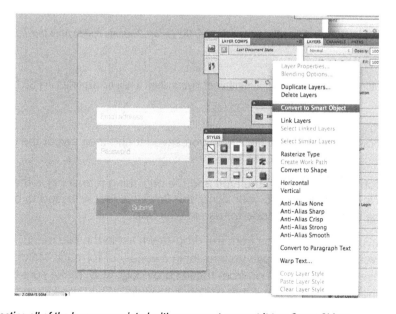

Figure 8-3. *After selecting all of the layers associated with your asset, convert it to a Smart Object*

Tip   Converting your layers to Smart Objects will allow you to edit your image without losing the original image data or quality.

After converting your layers to a Smart Object, you will see the new layer appear in the Layers panel.

5.   Select the new Smart Object you've just created from the Layers panel.

6.   Right-click to pull up the Export Contents of that as shown in Figure 8-4. Photoshop will ask you to choose a location for the file you are about to save. The new Smart Object file will have a .PSB extension.

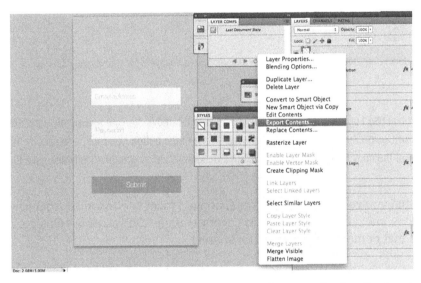

Figure 8-4. Export the contents of your Smart Object by selecting the Export Contents option from the drop-down menu

Tip   If a Smart Object was created from a number of layers, then it will be exported in PSB format.

7.   Find and open the exported file where you saved it and then select the layer with the asset you would like to save.

For our Submit button, we've removed the type and the only thing remaining is the actual button. Once this has been inspected and is to your liking, the Smart Object will need to be saved as a PNG so that it can then be imported into Xcode for use in your app.

8.   Select Save For Web Devices from the drop-down list in the File menu. You will be given the option to save your asset in a variety of formats. Make sure you choose the PNG-24 option from the list provided. Also, make sure to avoid using interlaced PNGs if that option is provided. The drop-down with the options, GIF, JPEG, PNG-8, and PNG-24 are shown in Figure 8-5.

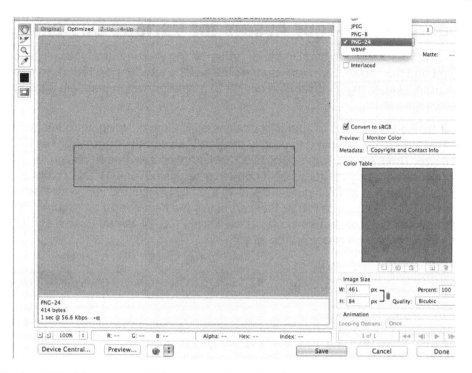

Figure 8-5. The Smart Object for export as a high-quality PNG-24. PNG-24 format preserves transparency

Tip   The PNG-24 option ensures the highest quality for your image. Apple recommends 24 as the standard bit depth for icons and images. There are 8 bits for each channel: red, blue, and green as well as an 8-bit alpha channel. Thus, the 24-bit PNG.

9.   After you select PNG-24, you should save the image in a memorable folder and call it "Submit_btn_off@2x." When you save the on state of the button, you want to maintain consistency in your naming conventions, so, your on or activated button name would be something along the lines of "Submit_btn_on@2x."

10.   If you haven't already created a new folder for your new assets, then do so. Choose this carefully, as it should be your location for all of the new assets you will be exporting. It is important that all of your assets live in the same folder.

And with that, you've just saved the first asset for your app. You will need to do this a few more times to get the hang of it, but once you do, it should go by quickly with each attempt.

This button we've just created, however, is a hi-res button. Let's now go through the process of how to scale the button down for our non-Retina devices.

Scaling and Saving Your Assets for Various Devices

Scaling and slicing your assets go hand in hand. \After slicing your images, you will need to save your 2x files first and then scale down making the files half the size for non-Retina screens. I prefer to scale down from a larger, higher resolution design to a smaller design because it maintains the integrity of the image better.

The process of saving your assets to a smaller scale is quite simple. Navigate to Image>Image Size to adjust the dimensions. We will need to modify the actual size of the button from its existing size to half its original size. There's been some discussion about dpi as it relates to design for iOS. It is my opinion that dpi does not really matter when it comes to designing for iOS. So, for this process we will leave the dpi as it stands at 72. Figure 8-6 shows the newly adjusted image size settings for our new non-Retina button. Navigate to File ➤ Save and save the new button as "Submit_butn_off.png." Follow the same instructions, as before in saving the file in PNG-24 format as well as the previously established naming convention and you'll be all set.

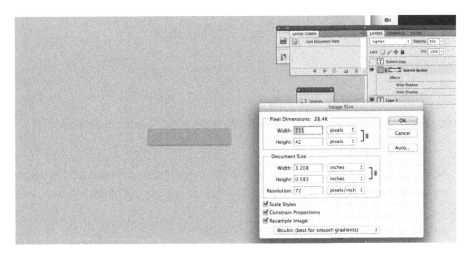

Figure 8-6. To create a non-Retina button, reduce the dimensions of the @2 button by 50%

To slice export and scale additional assets, follow the same process as outlined in the "Slicing Your Designs in Assets" section.

Slicing and scaling image selections for large PSDs can become tedious if you're going through the aforementioned slicing steps for a large number of assets. There are a number of tools available to assist designers in this process. Some of them are independent tools and others are plug-ins that work with Photoshop. Some of these are very popular. As always, try out a tool with a test PSD to ensure that it works the way that you need it to and make sure that it integrates with your workflow.

Other Asset Preparation Tools

If you are exporting a fair amount of images that are similar or even identical for some reason, you might be able to use the Export Layers to Files script in Photoshop. Select File ➤ Scripts ➤ Export Layers to Files and run the script. Photoshop will make sure that each layer of your document is saved in a different file. The file name will be whatever the name of the layer is so that you are able to identify it. In my opinion, this is a tool that has limited use cases so be careful when using this. You may want to make sure that your layer names are exactly what you want them to be before using this tool.

There are also more than a few third-party tools that can be used to assist with the asset preparation process for your iOS application. Some are executables and others are plug-ins that work with Photoshop. If you decide to use a third-party tool to assist with your asset preparation process, you will need to do some due diligence.

Here are a few things to look out for when considering using third-party tools for asset preparation:

- Perform tests with a few files first to ensure that the results are what you need.
- Make sure that the tool is updated regularly (a running log of bug fixes and updates will usually answer this question).
- The creator or company responsible for the tool should offer support or help for users.
- Read the reviews or feedback from users to see what others think. Reviews are a great indicator of how an app or plug-in performs.

Naming Your Assets

When creating assets for delivery to a developer, it is important to make sure that you maintain a consistent naming convention for your files. The following format for naming convention holds:

- Standard: <ImageName><device_modifier>.<filename_extension>
- Retina or High Resolution: <IMageName>@2x<device_modifier>.<filename_extension>

The <device_modifier> portion of the name is optional and not completely necessary. It can be a nice touch, however, if you're designing a universal app and want to indicate to your developer which asset belongs with a particular device.

When naming files, a good idea is to speak with your developer to find out if there is a preference but the following also can work as a guide, especially if you are creating an app with multiple form factors:

- iPhone – file.png or file~iphone.png
- iPhone Retina – file@2x.png or file@2x~iphone.png
- iPhone 5 – file-568@2x~iphone.png
- iPad – file~ipad.png
- iPad Retina – file@2x~ipad.png
- Third-party tools for exporting assets

Packaging Your Assets for Development

Once you've sliced, scaled, and exported your files into a folder, you should double check to make sure that everything is appropriately labeled for your developer. This takes the guesswork out of the developer trying to figure out where everything is. If you've created a Design Specifications Document, then you should include a section stating the naming convention you've used not only to name your files, but how you've organized them in the various folders. If your developer is fine receiving only a layered PSD document and does not want individually sliced PNGs, consider yourself lucky.

These days, more and more developers have ways of generating the slices they need and are familiarizing themselves with Photoshop. This removes some of the back and forth than can occur between developers and designers if, for instance, an image is a few pixels off. Whether or not your developer wants PNGs or a layered PSD, this is where it becomes important to make sure that your PSD has intuitively labeled layers. Also, some developers, while able to slice their own PSDs, may not be "hard-core" Photoshop experts. It is important not to rasterize or flatten the masks or layers before delivery to your developer so that he or she can edit a file if needed, without losing quality.

> **Tip**   Rasterizing an image converts it to a single layer and removes the ability to resize that image without losing quality.

Communication Is Key

Once your files have been labeled and packaged for delivery, you may also want to schedule a call or meeting with the developer to walk through nuances of your design or to explain actions and animations that may need additional clarification. While you will attempt to cover everything in your design specifications document, nothing beats a good old conversation. Send a copy of your document for your developer to review prior to your meeting and ask him or her to prepare any questions. No matter how clear you think your document is, it is likely that there will be questions. Any questions that are answered or clarifications that are made in your meeting will require you to update your document. Do so with those answers and send a new, updated version of your document to your developer so that the document can be referenced during development.

Another best practice is to make sure that your developer knows how to reach you in case he or she has follow-up questions. An e-mail address and phone number in the design specification document is helpful. Open lines of communication are a great way to take the guesswork out of the development process.

Summary

As you wrap up the design and ideation portion of your app, you will need to prepare your assets for delivery to your developer. A design specifications document is a great way to remove ambiguity from the development process. This is a document that you will create that will contain as much information about your app as possible. It should include details about the app; its purpose; how it will be used; and, more importantly, will tell your developer what to do with all of the assets you will be providing. You will offer details on color, font and text, interaction and animation if needed. You will then move onto slicing and scaling your asset for use in iOS. All of your assets, once sliced, must be exported as PNGs as they maintain transparency and offer great image quality. Once these assets are named and organized you will package them along with your design specifications document for handoff to your developer. If possible, you may want to follow up with an in-person conversation and provide some way for your developer to reach out to you. Whether you slice and scale your assets using the methods outlined in this chapter or using a third-party tool, adhere to these general guidelines to help smooth the transition from design to development.

Chapter 10

Design Best Practices and Mistakes to Avoid

You've taken your idea through ideation and now if you've delivered your app to a developer or perhaps even developed it yourself, you're ready to submit your app to the app store. Congratulations! This is a huge milestone and if you've followed the book through from the beginning to the end, you are hopefully pleased with the outcome. There was a lot of information to take in, so I've created a list for you to help you on your app design journey. It's pretty much a recap of all of the principles outlined in the book.

One of the most ignored aspects of app development is design. But hopefully with the tools and methods outlined in this book, I've helped to shed some light on the process. The interface or look and feel of your app is one of the most critical aspects of your app. Your audience will make its initial assessment of your app based on the interface in the screenshots you include in the app store. Some of the most simple and intuitive apps are the most popular.

While simplicity is important, it's critical to strike a balance between simplicity and functionality. Some apps are too overdesigned, including too many bells and whistles, which can take away from the overall functionality of the app. This is why referring back to your app statement is important. Keep the goal of the app top of mind while going through your design process and you should be just fine. The following sections break down the book into a helpful checklist of best practices and mistakes to avoid when designing your app.

Create an App Design Statement

An app design statement is the reason for your application. It's a short statement that you can easily remember that describes your application: the what; the why; and, most important, the how. Define your application and its intended audience. Keep this description short and be able to recite it to anyone who should ask. The app design statement that we created for our fictional Travel Light app was: "The Travel Light app will help frequent travelers by providing checklists to ensure that they pack only what they need for upcoming trips."

This statement may evolve and change as you create your app, but it's a good idea to memorize it and to update it should your idea change.

The HIG Is Your Design Bible; Use It

Apple's Human Interface Guidelines is like the Bible for designers and developers who are creating apps for iOS. In it, Apple has meticulously laid out its design principles and guidelines for designers and developers alike. Read it and reread it. Better yet, print a hard copy and keep it handy for when you have questions about pushing the boundaries of design for your app. If more designers and developers read the HIG, far fewer apps would be rejected from the app store.

Wireframing Is Important

Wireframing is the process of taking a concept and developing it fully on paper or some other method before the design process. Wireframing strips away all of the design elements and focuses on the user elements and the overall experience of the user as he or she interacts with your app. The wireframing process is critical to design and should actually be the first step in the design process. Oftentimes, the wireframing process can take some time, but this will save time once you move into the actual creative design process. Your wireframes will take you through every step of your application and will evolve over time as you define users, user stories, and user needs as you can see in Figure 10-1. Never underestimate the wireframing process. When they are complete and approved, your design process will go much smoother.

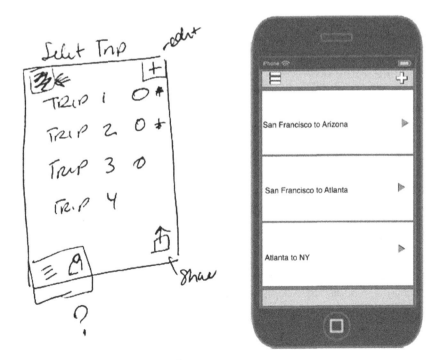

Figure 10-1. Sketched wireframes for a trip selection page of Travel Light app

UI vs. UX: There Is a Difference

User Interface and User Experience are different and it's good to know how they differ. UX or User Experience is what the user is actually experiencing as he or she journeys through the app. UI or User Interface is a visual representation of that experience. These two terms are often confused and misunderstood when it comes to app design. Understanding how they differ will also help your wireframing process.

Simplify!

Cluttered interfaces are confusing to users and can lead to confusion when using your application. Get rid of everything that's not critical. Be smart about how you implement functionality and don't give your users too many options! Simplicity is one of the hallmarks of iOS design principles. But, it is also a main tenet of mobile design in general. Overcomplicating your mobile design will cause confusion for users.

Utilize White Space

Some of the best apps use negatives spaces as a great component of the design process. Having space around the elements on the screen can be very important. It allows the eyes to focus on precisely what it needs to. Make specific elements the focus of your app as well as elements that are critical to the functionality of your application.

Be Aware of Changes to iOS 7

The HIG will outline the essentials of Apple's new operating system and its reliance on minimalism and flat design. Apply these principles to the design of your app. The iOS 7–specific information in the Human Interface Guidelines will help you understand the most sweeping changes to the OS since its release. It is also helpful to familiarize yourself with what others are doing in relation to the "flat design" trend and to understand how Apple has adapted this trend to suit the company's aesthetic.

Ask Why?

Take a look at your interface and ask yourself WHY a button is where it is. Determine how you can simplify the journey of the user. If there are additional steps that are not critical to the user's experience with the app, then remove them. Actually removing elements from the screen that are not absolutely necessary is a way to focus the user on the tasks at hand. If it's not critical to the user's journey, get rid of it.

Think Small

When designing your app, think about the fact that users will be interacting with your app on screens that are significantly smaller than a desktop screen. Designing for mobile and especially iOS means that space must be a consideration for each device. There are unique ways to interact with iOS devices, so keep them in mind.

The iPad Isn't Just a Big iPhone

If you're designing your app for the iPad there are specific design considerations that you must consider. For instance, consider how users will be interacting with your app on a larger device.

Fonts Are Important

Think about readability and how copy and text will appear on your device. Follow the Human Interface Guidelines, as they ere are specific with regard to fonts. Learn how fonts like Helvetica Neue (shown in Figure 10-2) are being utilized in iOS 7, and make sure that your copy is legible on the intended devices.

Helvetica Neue UltraLight
Helvetica Neue Light
Helvetica Neue Regular
Helvetica Neue Medium
Helvetica Neue Bold

Figure 10-2. Helvetica Neue is a popular flat design font

Provide Visual Feedback

Always let users know what's going on in your app. Providing feedback to users as a process is taking place is a great best practice. This includes the use of progress bars or the use of a spinner as in Figure 10-3 if an application is completing or is in the middle of a process. Your users want to know what's happening, so use these indicators to keep them apprised of what's happening within your app. When it comes to actions, visual feedback also helps. When a user taps on a button, creating and providing an "activated" or "on" state that is visually different from the "off" or "inactive" state lets the user know that the interaction has been received by the application. If there are specific ways that you would like to provide visual feedback for your user, be sure to mention these in the Design Specifications document so that your developer is aware of them.

Figure 10-3. A spinner lets the user know that a process is underway in an application

The User Is King (or Queen)

When designing your mobile app, you must always remember to put yourself in the position of your user. Create user stories and profiles and immerse yourself in that particular user's experience and tailor the app to fit that user. A user story is a profile of your ideal user and specific needs or requirements that he or she might have when using your app. Fleshing out these needs and prioritizing specific features based on user types will help you to narrow down your list of features. Understanding that you can't be everything to everyone will be helpful, too.

Design Patterns Are Your Friend

If you're still finding your way around the iOS interface or mobile in general, design patterns are a great way to understand well-established solutions for the interface design challenges for applications. Need a login or registration screen, or a way to display location-based search results? No problem. Design patterns can help and can take the guesswork out of problems and also speed up the overall design process.

Thumbs Rule

A popular mistake that can have lasting ramifications in your app is when you forget that thumbs rule. Remember that mobile users press or tap; they don't click. Therefore when designing your app, make sure that you're allowing adequate space for different sized fingers, especially thumbs. You will find that thumbs play an important role in app navigation. Think about where the important elements on the screen in your app will go, and make sure that they are within the reach of your users' thumbs. Apple's requirement for tappable areas is 44 x 44.

Hi- to Low-Res

Lots of designers tend to start with higher resolution designs and scale down. It will make your life a whole lot easier as you will be able to finalize and perfect details that are viewable in the larger versions but not the scaled-down ones. To be fair, some designers may prefer scaling up. However most of the designers I speak and work with prefer to scale down from higher resolutions to smaller ones.

Get 'Em in Quick

Intro screens and animations waste users' time. Keep your login and registration processes as brief as possible and get to the meat of your app sooner rather than later. Anything else is prohibitive. If you must have a walkthrough or a demo of your app, allow the user to bypass this process if he or she chooses to. Having a low barrier to entry is a great practice.

Test, Test, and Test Again

When creating your app, it's a good idea to get your app wireframes and designs into the hands of potential users as many times as possible. Take user feedback seriously before and even after you launch. It can make a huge difference. View your designs ON DEVICES where possible. I've mentioned some tools like LiveView and Scala that allow you to view your designs on the intended device so that you can allow for readability as it pertains to fonts *and* design. After your app has been developed, there is usually functional testing or quality assurance (QA) to ensure that the app behaves as it should. This should yield large issues that need to be addressed before you upload your app to the app store.

Software Will Help

Adobe Photoshop is the gold standard as far as design for apps and even web sites. If you're serious about design, learn it. There are tutorials on YouTube and entire books that cover Photoshop in greater detail than I do here.

Icons and Screenshots Are Important, Too

You rarely get a second chance to make a first impression. The user interface of your app is important, but so is your app's icon. It will be the sole means by which users will identify your app in the app store and on their devices. So it's important to make your icon as special as your app is. Apple provides guidelines for app icons as well, So, make sure that you follow them closely. Your app icon is required so put some serious thought into what this will look like. Your screenshots are the first view of your app that users will see. Include screenshots that will entice users to download your app.

Handoff and Communication

After you've designed your app and have everything ready to go, you will want to provide specific directions to your developer about special animations or gestures in your app. It's always a good idea to have an in-person conversation with your developer for an official handoff of the assets. As the designer, your work isn't done yet. You might want to create a document that your developer can refer to throughout the development process. This document will contain details that may not be immediately apparent from your layered PSD files. Information on fonts, colors, and sizes can all go into this document.

Summary

You've put a lot of work into the design of your app. You've created something out of nothing and brought it from just a thought, through ideation. When you hand off these files to your developer and the app is built, it will then become a unique creation that lives on hundreds of thousands of people's devices. Success isn't guaranteed, but if you've followed the Human Interface Guidelines and other documentation in this book, your app can be in the app store; and if it's really exceptional in terms of design and functionality, it could be featured with some of the other top apps in the store. Even if this doesn't happen, you should consider getting your app into the app store a great accomplishment.

Index

A

Abstract gestures, 41
Adobe Fireworks
    advantages, 101
    new features, 101
    structure, 101
    trip List PSD, 102
App designing
    Adobe Photoshop, 132
    desktop screen, 129
    fonts, 130
    handoff and
        communication, 132
    HIG, 128
    icons and screenshots, 132
    iOS 7, 129
    iPad, 130
    patterns, 131
    statement, 127
    testing, 132
    thumbs rule, 131
    UI *vs*. UX, 129
    Utilize White Space, 129
    visual feedback, 130
    wireframing, 128
App development
    asset preparation tools, 122
    Communication is Key, 124
    design specification document
        annotations, 114
        color information, 114
        fonts and types, 114
        user interaction (*see* User interaction (UI))
    naming assets, 123
    packaging assets, 124
    scaling and saving process, 122

slicing process
    asset finalization process, 117
    iOS, 117
    multiple layers, 118–119
    non-retina assets, 118
    PNG-24 format, 121
    retina, 118
    Smart Objects, 119
App discovery, 103–104
App icon, 106
App store
    app icons, 106
    app's page, 111–112
    conformation e-mail, 112
    iTunes account, 104
    launch image, 107
    new iOS 7 icon, 105
    newsstand cover
        icons, 107–108
    newsstand section
        code, 108
    promotional artwork, 110–111
    promotional screenshots, 108–109
Artwork, 110

B

Bars
    navigation, 17
    status bar, 16
    tab, 18
    toolbar, 17

C

Calculator app, 22
Calendar app's, 24
Color palette, 32

D

Design patterns
   design pattern box, 66
   list & table view patterns, 59
   registration and sign-up forms, 56
   searching and sorting feature, 62
   springboard/home screen
      patterns, 58
   tables
      image gallery, 62
      slide-out navigation, 61
      tabs, 60
   tip, tour, and walkthrough, 64
Developer's Conference in
      San Francisco, 9

E

eBay, 30

F

Flat design
   advantages, 31
   buttons, 34
   Color Palette, 32
   disadvantages, 31
   icons, 33
   iTunes Store, 36
   origin and use
      eBay, 30
      Twitter, 30
      Zune, 30
   principles of, 29
   space and templates, 34
   typography, 37
   usability, 38

G

Gestures
   abstract, 41–42
   consistency, 41
   direct manipulation, 41
   feedback, 42–43
   iOS devices
      double tap, 43
      drag, 44

      flick, 44
      pinch, 44
      shake, 44
      swipe, 44
      tap, 43
      touch and hold, 44
   iOS7
      swipe down, 45
      swipe right, 46
      swipe up, 45
   multi-touch experience, 40

H

Human Interface Guidelines (HIG), 10, 128

I

iOS 7
   bars
      navigation, 17
      status, 16
      tab, 18
      toolbar, 17
   design aesthetics, 9
   design-centric company, 9
   guiding principles, 10
   icons, 13
   springboard, 11
   stock apps
      buttons, 28
      Calculator app, 22
      calendar, 23
      color, 26
      designing applications, 21
      layers, 27
      mail, 22
      transparency and translucency, 26
      weather, 24
   table view elements, 20
   table views, 18
   typography, 12
iPads and iPhones design
   action sheet, 40
   app icon, 52
   e-commerce, 46
   four-finger swipe, 53–54
   gestures (see Gestures)

GUI kits, 39
icons
    LinkedIn homeand app
        store icons, 51
    sizes, 52
iPad 2, 46
iPad Mini, 46
iPad Retina, 46
launch image, 52
pinch, 54
popover, 48
screen resolution, 50–51
split view, 49
swipe, 53
targets, 50
UI elements, 39
universal app, 51
user interaction, 50
visual context, 50
iPhone Operating System (iOS) app
    app store exploration, 6
    category, 6
    comparison, 4
    download, 7
    idea, 2
    questions, 8
    share your idea, 3
    UI elements, 9
iTunes account, 104

J, K

Jonathan Ive, Apple's Creative Tsar, 10

L, M

Launch image, 107
Layer comps, 100

N, O

Navigation bar, 17

P, Q, R

Photoshop canvas, 94
PNG assets, 86
Prorotyping on Paper (POP), 82
PSD files, 111

S

Screenshots, 108–109
Skala tool, 86
Status bar, 16
Stock apps
    buttons, 28
    calculator app, 22
    calendar, 23
    color, 26
    layers, 27
    mail, 22
    transparency and translucency, 26
    weather, 24

T

Tab bar, 18
Toolbar, 17
Twitter bird logo, 30

U

User Experience (UX), 129
User interaction (UI)
    buttons, 116
    design specification document, 115
    font sizes, file names, and colors, 117
    login/signup, 115–116
User Interface (UI), 129

V

Visual assets, photoshop, 85
    Adobe Fireworks
        advantage, 101
        new features, 101
        trip List PSD, 102
    canvas display, 86
    gridlines & guides
        crop tools, 91
        3D tools, 93
        draw & type tools, 92
        main canvas, 88
        measuring tools, 91
        painting tools, 92
        retouching tools, 91
        selection tools, 90
        slice tools, 91

Visual assets, photoshop (*cont.*)
    symmetrical designs, 88
    tedious affair, 88
    tools panel, 89
    view and navigation tools, 93
iOS 7 design, 86
layer comps usage, 100–101
layers panel
    building blocks, 94
    change preference,
        property, 94
    group layer, 95
    multiple layers, 93
    natural structure, 94
    vectors, 95
photoshop history, 85
photoshop Setup, 87
PNGs assets, 86
registration/sign-in page creation
    background creation steps, 97
    branding colors, 95
    color picker panel, 95
    horizontal type tool, 98
    pastel-inspired color palette, 96
    sign-in screen with & without
        gridlines, 96
    travel light app sign-in screen, 97
    retina screen, 86
    select & edit trip page, 98
    user friendly, 86
    wireframes, 85

W, X, Y

Weather app's, 24
Wireframes
    definition, 69
    layout creation, 72
    process
        adding wireframe, 81
        clients, 83
        device outline, 73
        information architect, 74
        iPhone 5 and iPad mini stencil, 73
        POP, 82
        share wireframes, 81
        Travel Light, 75
        usability, 74
        use cases, 80
        user flow, 75
    tools, 71

Z

Zune, 30

Get the eBook for only $10!

Now you can take the weightless companion with you anywhere, anytime. Your purchase of this book entitles you to 3 electronic versions for only $10.

This Apress title will prove so indispensible that you'll want to carry it with you everywhere, which is why we are offering the eBook in **3 formats** for only $10 if you have already purchased the print book.

Convenient and fully searchable, the PDF version enables you to easily find and copy code—or perform examples by quickly toggling between instructions and applications. The MOBI format is ideal for your Kindle, while the ePUB can be utilized on a variety of mobile devices.

Go to www.apress.com/promo/tendollars to purchase your companion eBook.